DEDICATION

First, this book is dedicated to God, for where He has brought me from and where He is taking me. Second, this book is dedicated to my lovely wife, Della, who I passionately call my Prime Rib: thanks for being not only the love of my life but the backbone of our ministry and the glue that God uses to hold our family and our life together.

This book is also dedicated to my children, Kenneth, Kendall and Kristina, who were the motivating factors behind me putting together these stories — so that I could leave them a little insight into who their dad is, where he came from and what lessons he's learned that helped him overcome many obstacles in life.

My prayer is that they can learn from my past mistakes and victories, and also that, as they reflect on the stories I have left for them, they will be able to avoid the inevitable obstacles and pitfalls that Satan and life in general have in store for them. And lastly, this book is dedicated to all of the people in the stories who have added wisdom and strength to my life by their pain or their victories.

ABOUT THE AUTHOR

Ken Johnson was a Blue Chip All-American High School Football Player, and is a former Tulsa, Oklahoma police officer and Army Reserve Captain. He is now chaplain of the NFL Indianapolis Colts, a nationally known motivational and conference speaker, evangelist and recording artist. These accomplishments would be a dream come-true for most people, yet Ken's beginnings could have earned him the status of "All-American Failure." Born in Los Angeles to a heroin addict father and prostitute mother in the early 60s, mediocrity was a way of life. In 1968, Ken's family moved to the inner-city of Dallas, where Ken was raised on welfare and lived in a two bedroom apartment with nine people. Moving some eighteen times during a ten year period, Ken encountered the many challenges of inner-city living at a young age. His uncle, a pimp, pusher and so-called preacher, was the first role model Ken had in his life. A product of his environment, drugs, money and sports consumed Ken's life, and he began smoking marijuana and drinking alcohol in an attempt to fit in.

Ken thought he found two ways to pull himself and his family out of their bleak circumstances and poverty. First, he immersed himself in athletics, playing football, basketball and running track. His coaches became father-figures. Second, Ken felt he would succeed by imitating his uncle through dealing drugs and trying to be "Mr. Cool." Born with several God-given talents, including speed, size and strength, these athletic attributes helped Ken receive "Blue Chip All-American" recognition in high school football. Many people in Ken's life thought this was his way out of the inner-city. Ken was recruited by many of the major universities, but unfortunately, low academic scores and poor reading skills stood in the way of acceptance to a major college.

In the second game of his high school senior year, Ken

fractured the fifth vertebrae in his neck, which ended his season and threatened a future career in football. Recovery required being put in a halo brace and receiving schooling at home for four months. Ken worked hard to rehabilitate his neck and to get back into football shape. Though he had low academic scores, athleticism and determination earned him a scholarship to play football at the University of Tulsa. Ken excelled on the football field but struggled academically. Late night college parties and poor study habits caught up with him, and Ken was placed on academic probation by the university and suspended from the football team. As many young people have done, Ken strayed from God, but he remembered some of the messages his uncle used to preach.

In the summer of 1982, Ken's life took a drastic turn. While at a ROTC Training Camp, he met a young man named Bob Owens. Bob's total commitment to the Christian life made such an impact on Ken that he rededicated his life to Christ. Some of the Fellowship of Christian Athletes (FCA) members, who were Ken's teammates, went to the Tulsa football coaches on his behalf and asked for a second chance. FCA was instrumental in helping Ken to become more disciplined and nurturing him both spiritually and academically. Second Corinthians 5:17 became a reality in his life: "Therefore if any man be in Christ, he is a new creature: Old things are passed away; Behold, all things are become new."

Strengthened by his renewed faith, he became an active member of FCA. That same year, Ken married his girlfriend Della, received his commission as 2nd Lieutenant in the U.S. Army Reserves, and earned his Bachelor of Science degree in Education—graduating with honors. During this time, Ken began speaking and singing at FCA events in the surrounding area and dedicated his life to being a positive role model for his peers and family. A knee injury prevented Ken from pursuing a professional football career, and he decided to become a police officer in Tulsa, Oklahoma. Sensing a strong call of God in his life, he was ordained through AZUSA Fellowship, Inc., out of Higher Dimensions Evangelistic Center in Tulsa and under the leadership of Bishop Carlton Pearson.

During this time, Ken was the chaplain for the Black Officers Coalition and president of Police Officers for Christ. He organized the ministry SHARE (Stand, Help And Rid Evil), feeding over 1000 people each month, providing toys to over 2500 children at Christmas, and issuing over 1000 fans during the hot summers in Tulsa. Ken was also able to assist his family in Dallas.

After serving six years as a police officer and minister and feeling despondent about the plight of today's youth, Ken felt that God was calling him to the ministry full time. Accepting the call, he moved his wife and two small children, Kendall and Kristina, to Indianapolis where he took the position of State Urban Director for FCA of Indiana. As the Director, Ken worked with inner-city youth to provide food, clothing and Christian role models for the community, and he also spoke and sang to the congregations of many churches around Indiana and surrounding states.

However, God was calling Ken to be more active on a national level, and feeling the need to use his gifts of evangelism more effectively, he left FCA to begin the Helping Hands Group, Inc. Today, Ken travels across the country with Ken Johnson Enterprises, to groups such as: the National Student Council Leadership Conference, PRIDE, DARE, Character Counts, and to the school administrations and staff and students at hundreds of schools and colleges. He has also spoken at National and Regional Promise Keepers events and to many other groups. Whether young or old, white or black, rich or poor, all are touched by the Hope Dealer, Ken Johnson, through Ken Johnson Enterprises.

CONTENTS

JOURNEY TO EXCELLENCE
Lessons From the Heart of a Father

INTRODUCTION
Excellence or Mediocrity? Your Choice

Philippians 4:8: *"Finally brothers, whatever is true, whatever is noble, whatever is right, whatever is pure, whatever is lovely, whatever is admirable. If anything is excellent or praiseworthy, think about such things."*

- Webster's New World Dictionary defines excellence as: the fact or condition of excelling; superiority; surpassing goodness, merit, etc.
- Vince T. Lombardi said, "The quality of a person's life is in direct proportion to their commitment to excellence, regardless of their chosen field of endeavor."
- Rev. Dr. Martin Luther King said, "If a man is called to be a street sweeper, he should sweep streets even as Michelangelo painted, or Beethoven composed music, or Shakespeare wrote poetry. He should sweep the streets so well that all the Host of Heaven and earth will pause to say, 'Here lived a great street sweeper who did his job well.'"
- Mario Andretti said, "Desire is the key to motivation, but it's the determination and commitment to an unrelenting pursuit of your goal — a commitment to excellence — that will enable you to attain the success you seek."

We are what we repeatedly do. Excellence then is not an act but a habit. We are a sum total of our experience, so live your life to be the best that you can be. It's a funny thing about life: if you refuse to accept anything but the very best, you will very often get it.

Excellence is going far beyond the call of duty, doing more than others expect — this is what excellence is all about.

Excellence comes from striving, maintaining the highest standards, looking after the smallest detail, and going the extra mile. Excellence means doing your very best, in everything, in every way. I want you to know that excellence can be attained, if you:

- **Care more than others think is wise.**
- **Risk more than others think is safe.**
- **Dream more than others think is practical.**
- **Expect more than others think is possible.**
- **Give more than others think is best.**
- **Love more than others think is necessary.**

I love what Thomas A. Edison said: "If there's a way to do it better, find it." Thomas Wolfe said, "If a man has a talent and cannot use it, he has failed. If he has a talent and uses only half of it, he has partly failed. If he has a talent and learns some-how to use the whole of it, he has gloriously succeeded, and won a satisfaction and a triumph few men ever know."

As a former police officer, and presently as an evangelist and inspirational speaker who travels across the United States speaking in schools, businesses, and civic organizations, also preaching in churches, prisons and to special groups, I see first-hand how the devil has tricked many people into believing that they are less than what God has intended them to be. So many of God's holy, chosen ambassadors are settling for mediocrity when God is calling them to excellence.

Webster's New World Dictionary defines mediocrity as: neither very good nor very bad; ordinary; average; just good enough.

I believe that the enemy of best is not *worst*, but "*good enough*." So many people are satisfied with just being good enough, and this is dangerous for Christians because God never called us to be just good enough. He tells us in Matthew 5:13-16 to be "salt and light." In Philippians 3:14, He tells us to "press towards the goal of he upward call," and in Ephesians 6:13, He says therefore put on the "full armor of God, so that when the day of evil comes, you may be able to stand your ground. And after you have done everything to stand. Stand!"

If ever there was a time when God's people needed to stand against mediocrity, it's now. According to a survey conducted by Dr. James Dobson starting in 1990, one out of every four children live in poverty, the elderly account for 35% of the poor, and 3,000,000 homeless people try to make do with only 100,000 beds.

In the great country of America, the most segregated hour is eleven o'clock on Sunday morning. We can work together, live in the same neighborhoods, attend sporting events, but when it comes to worship we seem to stay separated. Many Muslims, Yahweys, Klu Klux Klansman, and Neo-Nazi groups are running rampant spreading prejudice and racism and the church seems to sit idly by and says and does nothing.

In 1991, an estimated 400,000 people died from Aids. By 1992, we were already out of beds to handle all the Aids cases, and where are God's people? In 1980, when there was less sex education in our classrooms, four million teenagers reported venereal diseases. Now, in the age of safe sex and much more sex education, we have over 20 million reported cases every year. More than 1.5 million teenage girls between the ages of 12 and 17 become pregnant each year—98% of these pregnancies are out of wedlock and 78% of these young women become pregnant again within a year. Over half of these girls have abortions, which equates to 4400 each day and over 30 million since 1973. In the United States if ever there were a time for Christians to stand up and fight it is now. According to that same survey:

- **Every 8 seconds a child drops out of school.**
- **Every 26 seconds a child runs away from home.**
- **Every 46 seconds a child is abused or neglected.**
- **Every 7 minutes a child is arrested for a drug offense.**
- **Every 36 minutes a child is killed or injured by a gun.**
- **Every day 135,000 children bring guns to school.**

There are 83 people each minute, 49,800 people each hour, and 119,520 people each day who will go into eternity lost, dying without ever knowing Jesus Christ as their Savior. Imagine nearly one million people per week going into eternity lost. My question is: what are you doing to make an impact for God in these areas? We must do all we can to turn our world back around towards Jesus Christ! It is time we had a higher level of expectation from our children and from ourselves. I have seen firsthand that children give you what you model. They don't do what you say; they do what they see you do. A parent who drinks, smokes or uses foul language but tell their children not to do so are good examples of this. One of the Promise Keeper's conference themes was "Raising the Standard." We raise the standard when we pursue excellence in God by modeling out the love of Christ in our daily lives.

In the pages of this book I plan to take you on one man's journey through the first half of life. Bob Buford wrote a book called "Half Time" and that is where this book takes my life, through the first two quarters. My prayer is that through my life others may be touched and reach for God's Kingdom. God has touched me and helped me break the chain of failure in my family. My prayer is this book will inspire and equip others to do the same.

CHAPTER ONE

The Chicken and the Eagle Story: Fly High or Cluck Low

"Be on your guard; stand firm in your faith; be men of courage; be strong."

I Corinthians 16:13

Once there were some men climbing in the mountains. They came across a large nest, and in the nest they found some eggs. These climbers were chicken farmers, so they decided to take one of the eggs back to their farm to see if the mother hen could hatch it along with the other eggs. Once the egg was inside the coop, the mother incubated all the eggs, including the one brought to her from the mountains. Several weeks went by and all the eggs began to hatch. Out came cute little baby chicks, but the egg the mountain climbers brought in still had not hatched.

One day, the egg began to move, cracked open, and out came an ugly little baby eagle. The baby eagle looked like a sick puppy with its hair falling out! The mother hen looked at the baby eagle and said, "You sho' is a ugly chicken."

And the baby eagle responded, "Well you're ugly too!"

The mother hen grabbed him and said, "You can't talk to me that way; you have to conform. You have to do what every-one else is doing."

To that the eagle thought, "I don't feel like a chicken or look like a chicken, but I must be a chicken because I'm here with all these other chickens. So I'll conform and try to get along." The little eagle tried to walk, talk and act like a chicken, but something was wrong. Since eagles eat meat, what do you think he did when he got hungry? He tried to eat chickens.

The mother hen was back pecking on his head again. "Chickens don't eat chickens," she said. "Chickens eat bird-seed."

The little eagle said, "I hate birdseed! I hate it here!" He looked up to the sky and said, "Sometimes I want to fly. I close my eyes and dream that I am flying." Just as he looked up, he saw a great bird flying and said, " I want to fly just like that bird. I believe that I can fly! I want to fly like that bird."

The mother hen and all the chickens told him, "You'll never fly like that. That high flying bird is an eagle, one of the greatest birds in the world. You're just an ugly chicken."

The little eagle lowered his head and said, "I quit, I give up," and decided to starve himself to death. He lost all hope of leaving the chicken coop, but as he lay down to die, the big eagle swooped down in front of the chicken coop because he wanted some chicken.

As the big eagle looked around, surveying lunch, he saw what resembled a little eagle lying in the back of the coop. He thought to himself, "Why isn't that eagle having lunch? Maybe he's eaten too much and he can't get up."

All the chickens ran to the back of the coop, screaming, "The eagle is here! The eagle is here! He's come to eat us!" The eagle again thought to himself: "That cannot be an eagle in there with all those chickens because if it were he'd be having lunch right now!"

As he examined the bird more intently, he realized it really was an eagle, and he yelled toward the back of the coop, "Hey you lying down over there, come here!"

The little eagle jumped to attention and began to walk to the front of the chicken coop. He remembered his dream of flying as he looked up and saw that big eagle. He remembered saying to himself, "I believe I can fly!" As he continued to walk toward the eagle, all the chickens told him not to go, saying, "That's an eagle, and he's going to eat you because you're the ugliest one in here." The little eagle pushed passed his fears and the criticism of the chickens. He clung to his hope and the dreams that he had of flying one day. Even though he was afraid, he kept moving forward. Something deep down inside let him know that everything would be okay. He was walking toward his destiny and purpose.

As he got to the edge of the coop, he looked up and the big eagle asked, "What are you doing in there?"

The smaller bird answered, "I'm a chicken and I'm here with all the rest of the chickens."

The big eagle stated, "You're *not* a chicken! You're an eagle!"

After arguing for a little while, the big eagle grabbed the little eagle and took off into the sky. The little eagle didn't want to go because he was afraid to leave the coop, even though he had that dream of flying. He had never flown before and a part of him was afraid to leave the coop.

He screamed, "No I don't want to go!"

But the more he screamed, the higher the big eagle took him. They flew higher and higher until they found a high cliff on the edge of a great mountain.

The little eagle screamed, "Hold me, hold me! I'm gonna fall!"

To that, the big eagle stated, "You can fly. All you have to do is try."

The little eagle responded, "If I try to fly, I might die."

"No," the big eagle said. "You won't die if you try to fly. All you have to do is try."

The little eagle began to respond again, "But I can't f..." Before he could get the word "fly" out of his mouth, the big eagle pushed him off the cliff. The little eagle fell, tumbling uncontrollably until a big gust of wind rushed under his wings and pushed him upward.

As he began to soar, he realized he was flying, and it was so beautiful! He began to say with excitement, *"I can fly, I can fly!"*

The big eagle swooped down next to him and said, "You were meant to fly like this." They then flew up and perched on the same cliff the young eagle had been pushed from. As the little eagle looked around, he was in awe of all the things he had never seen before.

The big eagle looked at him and said, "Do you know what your problem has been?"

"No, what?" the little eagle responded.

"You've been down there with those chickens so long that you never learned about your true purpose! God sent me by to tell you that your purpose is to fly high above the clouds, not to be stuck in a coop or cluck like a chicken anymore," the big eagle said. "And don't you ever forget it!"

Sometimes, like the chickens, we find ourselves in a world that is trying to make us conform to mediocrity. We try to fit in, but the more we try, the more we realize how meaningless it is to try, and we often want to give up. The more we try to better ourselves and try to make this world a better place to live, the more we are criticized and rejected by sinful people. But it is our God-given duty to push past the criticism and walk toward our destiny and purpose, to be *world shakers and disciple makers.*

God is calling us upward, out of our comfort zones, to take us to new heights, to dream big dreams, and to never lose hope. The purpose of this book and the stories in it are to remind you that it is time to spread your wings and fly high and not to cluck low like a chicken anymore. The stories in this book will convey important points, just as the Chicken Eagle story did, and I pray that you will learn many valuable lessons as you read. If God has spoken to you like He has spoken to me in many areas of my life, I hope and pray that you will not let your fears and anxieties strip you of the courage to fly. ***Do not follow where the path may lead, but go instead where there is no path and leave a trail.*** Don't ever forget that leaders are like eagles: they don't belong to a flock and you find them one at a time. It takes courage to push yourself to places that you have never been before, to test your limits, to break through barriers, but remember there is always room at the top! Ask yourself, "In what areas of my life do I need to stop thinking like a chicken but soaring like an eagle?"

All eagles have courage. It's a special kind of knowledge: the knowledge of how to fear what ought to be feared and how not to fear what ought not to be feared. From this knowledge comes an inner strength that inspires us to push onward in the face of great difficulty. What can seem impossible becomes possible with courage. Courage is doing what you're afraid to do. Eddie Rickenbacker, the great military pilot said, "There can be no courage unless you're scared."

"All the significant battles are waged within the self," says Sheldon Kopp. "For God hath not given us the spirit of fear; but of power, and of love, and of a sound mind" (2 Timothy 1:7). God is calling us to be ready for action. He tells us to "be strong and courageous, because you will lead these people to inherit the land He swore to their forefathers to give them" (Joshua 1:6). If we are going to be the eagles that God is calling us to be, we must be courageous. As God's people, may we never forget that "we can't lose with the stuff we use."

My high school football and track coach used to always say, "winners never quit and quitters never win and we're not born winners, we're not born losers, we're born choosers." You have a choice every day how you choose to play. I have taken this philosophy and made it a major part of my life. I've added to the statement, "every choice that we make will have a positive or negative affect on our life and those who may be following us." So who's in your life helping you choose better and who are you helping to choose better?

CHAPTER TWO

Wait On God

"Even the youths shall faint and be weary, and the young men shall utterly fall; but they that wait upon the Lord shall renew their strength; they shall mount up with wings as eagles; they shall run and not be weary; and they shall walk and not faint."

Isaiah 40:30-31

The preceeding passage is my life scripture. Everything that I discover about the characteristics of eagles, I am trying to develop in my own life. The eagle is the United States of America's national symbol, and the eagle is on our currency. The Eagle Scout is the highest honor among the Boy Scouts, and the eagle is often identified with strength, courage, honor, truth, and faithfulness. If you come to my home, you will discover that I have a great passion for what eagles represent. In fact, since 1993, I have been collecting eagles. My home is filled with all kinds of eagles, and the collection is growing to the point that my wife Della has threatened to hurt me if I bring one more home. I have eagles crafted from glass, wood, brass, marble, bronze, and more.

There are many characteristics about the eagle to admire. While there are too many to mention here, some of the special features include: Eagles can grow as large as three feet in body length and can carry up to 90 pounds in their talons. They have up to a seven-foot wingspan, and they can soar to over 10,000 feet in the air and then dive at more than 100 miles per hour. Eagles don't just flap their wings; they soar on the currents of the air. They use the same winds to soar higher that push lesser birds down. The eagle is one of the few birds that is not afraid to fly in the eye of a hurricane. The eagle knows where to find safety in the midst of the storm, and the eye of the storm is where the eagle finds peace. He flies up through the eye while winds swirl around him and comes out on top of the storm. While other birds and animals run away from the storm, the eagle uses adversity as opportunity.

Eagles are extremely devoted creatures, and they will stay united with their mate for life. At times, an eagle must retire to a solitary place for renewal. As a result of hunting, the eagle's wings become soiled and their claws become dull so that they can't grasp their prey. Over time, their beaks become brittle and they can't strip their food. In the solitary place, the eagle pulls out his soiled wing feathers, extracts his dull claws, and smashes all the brittle parts from its beak. During the re-growth process, the eagle's mate brings food. Some time later, the eagle emerges in a renewed condition, stronger than before! The eagle mounts up with wings that are no longer burdened down by the dirt of the world. His claws and beak have re-grown and he is eager to conquer the challenges and obstacles of life.

In similar fashion, every new creature in Christ experiences renewal as he lays aside his old self, gaining strength as he leans on the Lord. Through the example of the eagle, God has shown me how I can find peace in my storms and be renewed in the promises and assurances of His word. One familiar saying I have always heard is: "God may not come when you want him, but he's always right on time." So wait on God! And in his time He will give you everything you need while equipping you to do what He has called you to do.

During the first quarter of my life I did not embrace the lesson of the eagle. It took many unpleasant experiences and failures along with God strategically placing people into my life's journey to get me to an Eagle mentality.

Like the Eagle's mate bringing food, nourishment in time of renewal, God brought people into my life during that first quarter to systematically lead me to a relationship with him.

CHAPTER THREE

My Story:
All Things Work For the Good; Just Hang in There

"And we know that in all things God works for the good of those who love him who have been called according to His purpose."

Romans 8:28

In some books I have read, people go into great detail outlining all the bad things that they have done to show where God brought them from and how good God is at saving the unsavable. I love to hear and to read these great testimonies, but I don't want to give Satan any glory in the areas of my past and the details that I feel God has called me to share with you. I do not wish to justify or glorify my past only to show that the surpassing mercy and grace of our Lord and Savior Jesus Christ can cover a multitude of sins. I have found that most people justify their current failures by using their past mistakes as an excuse. I will try to use this book to give some information on who, what, where, when and why of my own evolution, and I want to show how Jesus' power, through his Holy Spirit, is the key to changing our world and people in our world for the better.

Obstacle or Opportunity

This story is about an inner-city boy who is on a journey to excellence. Each time I share this story, I am amazed and overwhelmed by what God can and will do for those who place their faith, hope and trust in Him.

My story begins in 1960, in General Hospital in Los Angeles, California. I was born to Leonard Johnson and Barbara Delores Johnson, a 19 year-old mother who was raised in a very dysfunctional family. Her dad was an alcoholic, ex-con and an abusive father. Not having proper guidance and discipline, she became a very wild and confused young lady. I don't know much about my dad but what I've been told. However, I can remember that he was about five years older than my mother and a professional landscaper, but he was also a heroin addict and very abusive.

My aunt told me some of the things that go along with the bits and pieces of what I can remember from my early childhood. My mother, Barbara, ran away from her parents' home in Dallas, Texas at the age of 14 because she didn't want to live with a drunk and abusive father. She stayed away for four months and no one knew where she was. I am told this was a common occurrence with my mom. After returning home, she and her older brother Charles remained in those same conditions until the age of 16 and she could no longer take the pressure. She moved to Los Angeles to live with her Aunt Mae Mae, who recalls extreme difficulties in raising Mom. At the age of 17, my mother met and married Leonard Johnson.

By the time I was born, my mother was 19 years old and had two other sons, Leonard Jr. and Donald. Donald was killed after an alleged accident. The story goes that Leonard Sr. threw Donald in the air while playing catch, striking his head on the ceiling and killing him. Understandably, my mom doesn't like to discuss or talk about her past, and consequently, I have mixed emotions about sharing this with anyone. A part of me feels that it is no one's business, that what happened in the past should be left there, and another part feels that I must tell the truth to show just how good God is and how far he has brought me.

By the time my mom was 24 years old, three more children had been born: Perry, Donna (the only girl), and Curtis (Randy). My earliest memory of my family was the day we brought Randy home from the hospital. I can remember what I felt at the time was a big house. I can even remember the address: 895 E. 42nd Street. It is amazing the things you remember and the things you forget about from your past. I remember some good times, like Christmas, when we would get boxes of toys. I remember my first bike. As I attempted to learn to ride, I fell many times on my knees, arms and hands. I got very bloody but never stopped until I got it down. I can remember my godmother taking me for pancakes at IHOP and window shopping. I can remember going to church and seeing my mother cry as she and my aunts were in front of the church with all of us kids, crying about something. I remember playing cowboys and Indians and cops and robbers with my brothers. I remember my older brother hitting my sister in the head with a rock because she was always getting us in trouble. After the rock incident, there were no more episodes like that. We were at Aunt Mae Mae's house at the time, and my sister was her favorite. Nobody would tell who threw the rock, so we were all whipped with an extension cord. I also remember the really bad times, like being awakened in the middle of the night by the fights between my parents. I remember the times my dad would come home so drunk and high and beat my mom and us kids. This is the result of being an alcoholic as well as a heroin addict.

The Night When Things Changed Forever

One night was a lot different than many other nights of fighting, however. I was awakened by sounds of what I thought were fire crackers. As I walked down the stairs, I could see my older brother lying on the bathroom floor as if he were drunk or half asleep. He had a syringe laying next to him and he was trying to sit up but couldn't. As I turned the corner, walking thru the kitchen to the living room, I saw my mother holding a pistol. One of the windows was shattered. Before I could say anything, my father attempted to climb back through the window and my mother shot him again. My mother was screaming, "How could you do it? How could you do that to your own son?" My father had just shot up Leonard, Jr. (11 years old) with heroin. After the police had come, the ambulance took my father and brother to the hospital. My mother was taken to a mental hospital as she had literally gone insane right in front of our eyes.

We were taken to live with Aunt Mae Mae, who was a cruel and hateful woman. She used prescription drugs to get up in the morning, keep her up during the day, and to help her sleep at night. I have never met a woman who took so many different types of pills. Maybe that is why she had those continual mood

swings; maybe that is why she was so cruel. She had two children, Cassandra and Samuel (Sam). Cassandra was very nice
to us, but Sam was physically and verbally abusive. Let's just
say that living in their home was a very unpleasant experience.
When we asked where our mother was, they would always reply
that she was in the hospital and that she was sick. They would
say the same about my father. I later discovered that Mom had
a nervous breakdown and Dad was recovering from gunshot
wounds.

One day, a ray of hope shined into our bleak existence.
Leonard, Jr. and my mom came to take us from Aunt Mae Mae's
and back to our home. Leonard had special medication and had
been in the hospital to help him overcome the heroin addiction,
but he was never quite the same again.

The Big Move To Dallas

When my father was released from the hospital, no
charges were brought against him and he came back to live with
us. After two months, another late-night fight erupted, and the
next day our mother withdrew us from school and we were on
a bus headed for Dallas, Texas. Two days later, we were met
by my grandfather, Will Earl Thompson, who took us to live
with my uncle Charles Thompson (Uncle Bill), who was a pimp,
drug pusher and a so-called preacher. He was married with two
children, and he and his family lived in a one-bedroom apartment! When we moved in with them, there were 10 of us in that
apartment for over a year. My mom would work odd jobs and
do whatever she could to help assist with whatever was needed.
I know several men were in and out of her life during this time.
I can remember her saying many times, "Whatever I have to do
to feed my babies, that's what I have to do." We later moved in
with my Grandmother Ellisse and her new husband, Grandpa
Jones, for a short time until we got our own place. It seemed

that we moved once or twice each year, living where we could until evicted to go through the same process again and again and again. It seems like we lived out of boxes.

We had been in one house for a year, and Mom seemed to be getting on her feet. I remember having a brand new red bike to help throw papers on my paper route. Leonard, Jr. ran back and forth from Dallas to Los Angeles and was constantly in trouble for fighting and disturbing behavior. He finally dropped out of school. After being in LA a year, my father couldn't control him, so he came back and asked to live with us again. My mom gave Leonard, Jr. rules he had to abide by and he replied, "If I can't live here the way I want to, nobody will," and the next day, he burned the house down. I guess those drugs really fried his brain.

I can remember the police catching him, and I can vividly see my mom beating him and the police pulling her off him. Leonard, Jr. was arrested and put in juvenile detention until he turned eighteen. Once released, he continued his destructive behavior, stealing, raping women, and many other things, which led to prison at least five times. He is now serving a 50-year sentence in Texas with no chance of parole.

Leonard, Sr. remarried and was shot and killed by his new wife. My mom would not allow us to attend the funeral, but Mae Mae sent pictures.

From that point on, and over a period of five years, we were back in that same pattern of moving twice a year. We would find an apartment or rental house, stay there until evicted, and again my mom would do whatever she could to make sure we had food to eat and a roof over our heads.

The Good, The Bad, The Ugly

We were on welfare and extremely poor. I don't remember getting a new pair of tennis shoes until my coach in junior high bought me a pair. I remember shopping at Goodwill and other second-hand stores. By this time, my mom had been through many relationships and I was going into high school when a ray of hope in the form of a 6'4", 300 lb. man by the name of Big Lou (Louis Shropshire) came into my mom's life. He would later become my step-dad, but he literally had to fight his way into our home.

I had become a product of my environment. I was racist, extremely vulgar, used marijuana, and drank alcohol almost daily. I was promiscuous, and I had no respect for myself or anyone else. I became just like my uncle, who considered himself a pimp, pusher and preacher. He would sell dope, pimp, and prostitute the women he would preach to on Sunday morning. Consequently, I had a warped perception of Christians and Christianity. I was taught that you could live like hell Monday through Saturday as long as you gave Sunday to God. I can even remember walking down the aisle when the preacher called for all those who didn't want to go to hell but wanted to go to heaven, praying the sinner's prayer and asking the Lord to come into my life. I was crying and everyone in the church seemed to be so happy for me. Even my mom, brothers and sister.

Bringing a child into the world doesn't raise that child. We have to be nurtured and disciplined. By this time in my life I had two consistent male role models in my life: Uncle Bill and Big Lou. Uncle Bill turned me on to drugs, and he gave me my twisted perspective on women and relationships and a pimp mentality. He told me life was a game and the game was about making money. He said money was god.

Exodus 20:4-6 says: "You shall not make for yourself an idol in the form of anything in heaven above or on the earth beneath or in the waters below. You shall not bow down to them or worship them, for I, the Lord your God, am a jealous God, punishing the children for the sins of the fathers to the third and fourth generation of those who hate me, but showing love to a thousand generations of those who love me and keep my commandments."

My uncle would preach on Sundays, but I guess he did not come across this passage of scripture.

Hope vs. Hell

I want to say here, now that I have matured, I see how warped and destructive that mentality was. I see now that the sins of the father are truly passed down from one generation to the next if you don't have the Lord to stop the curse. Uncle Bill, after being in and out of prison, continued his reckless lifestyle too. His wife eventually divorced him and he became addicted to the very drugs he would sell to others. He was arrested for armed robbery and attempted murder and convicted to serve 70-years in a Texas prison with no hope of parole but believe God is going to work a miracle in his case.

Big Lou, on the other hand, worked many, many hours, and he took care of five kids who were not even his. He wasn't a Christian man, but he was the warmest, funniest, most compassionate man I had ever met. He was like a big teddy bear. He worked daily, brought his check home to Mom, and was the only man that could put up with my mom's continual mood swings. He helped instill a work ethic in me, encouraging me to eat properly and get proper rest. I can still hear him saying, "Son, if you go to bed before 9:30 p.m., you'll gain weight and be more alert.

Big Lou had to fight his way into our home by physically handling a man who was attempting to use my mom in a ring of prostitution. That man broke into our apartment one night where he was met by Big Lou, who beat him with a table, and held him until police came and arrested the guy for breaking and entering and assault. I consider Big Lou a real man's man, and he has been with my mom over thirty years. I can truly say that a lot of the good that is in me has come from the example Big Lou set. Today he and mom are married and he is an elder in his church and a member of the male chorus. Big Lou accepted the Lord at my Grandfather's funeral where I officiated. The topic was "Hell No, You Don't Want to Go". When I gave the altar call everyone in the funeral home, including he and my mom, came forward and accepted the Lord. I believe that the life that Della and I led before them truly gave them hope that *it doesn't matter where you come from to decide where you can go.*

In 1993, shortly after my grandfather's funeral, Big Lou and my mom got married after being together over twenty years and still together. My mom is the church mother in a small Baptist church in Dallas, and Big Lou is an elder and head of the men's ministry. God still performs miracles, after serving twenty-one years in prison in Texas, Uncle Bill was released in 2003 with fifty years left to complete his sentence and is leading worship and preaching occasionally in the same church my mom and Big Lou attend. God showed grace and mercy to all of my family who truly repented and turned from their wicked ways. What miraculous thing are you believing God for? If he did this for my family he can surely do it for whatever you're believing for.

Athletic Influence

I was a pretty good athlete, and all we did was get high, party, play basketball, and play sandlot football. By this time I was involved in organized team sports, however, and I excelled in everything and anything I put my hands to. That is where I got the name Bird. One day in junior high, I was running in a track meet and they said my feet were going so fast it looked as if I was flying. I always enjoyed singing too, and that night at an awards ceremony I sang the national anthem. When I got back to the table, one of the young ladies said, "He runs and sings like a bird," and the name stuck.

I can remember singing in the choir on Sunday with marijuana in my pocket while making eyes at the girls with lustful thoughts in my mind and heart. Even though I was popular, cool, and I thought I had it all together, I was clueless. I was a bird alright, but at this time during the first quarter I was "stuck on stupid" and a chicken in a coop. I had all the characteristics of the eagle, but was sulking in the dirt with all the other chickens.

CHAPTER FOUR

High School:

Good, Better, Best

*"Do not merely listen to the word, and so deceive yourselves.
Do what it says"*

James 1:22

A totally new and exciting horizon was presented to me in high school. The land of opportunity, the land of milk and honey, was Woodrow Wilson High School, which was 60% white, 30% black and 10% Hispanic. From my freshman year on, I was the big man on campus. I played on the varsity football team as well as running track. I sat on the bench in basketball. High school for me was the time I took cool to another level. Who you were and what you did meant everything. I received all my recognition, status and a sense of who I was from athletics and trying to be a man's man. Athletics was my god, coaches were my preachers, and my fellow athletes were my fellow congregants and fellow disciples. Almost anything my coaches told me to do, I would do; and anything that would impress my so-called friends, I would try.

During football and basketball season was the only time I showed respect to my teachers and white teammates. I knew that the only way that I would get out of the ghetto was to get a scholarship, and my coaches continually reinforced that as well. My coaches told me that I had to have a good reputation and be well liked to get an opportunity to go to college. They said that I had the ability to not only play college ball but make it all the way to the pros. But there were other gods and preachers in my life. Thank God for my coaches, and my teachers who never gave up on me. Without them fighting for me the world would have totally defeated me.

These gods were in conflict with the God of excellence. They were the gods of mediocrity and the gods of my sinful nature. They were in constant conflict with one another. There were dope dealers my uncle introduced me to, my get high and party friends, those promiscuous girls who told me what I wanted to hear and used sex as a tool to trap a man like a fly in the web of a spider. This low level of expectation that I had for myself due to my lack of self esteem and improper biblical role models in my life began to make me a destructive person. On the one hand, I felt in control and on top of everything; and on the other hand, I felt inadequate and unable to accomplish anything great. Which god would I serve? "A double-minded man is unstable in all his ways" (James 1:8). Because I spent more time with the gods that appealed to my lower nature, I was pulled down even though I tried to balance my life by working hard, lifting weights, running and conditioning my body—mediocrity became my standard. I was *stuck on stupid*.

I did only enough to get by when it came to academics. I saw academics merely as a qualifying necessity to my athletic endeavors. I understood that if I did not pass in class I could not play sports, and consequently, I did just enough to pass and not enough to excel. I saw so-called Christians as being hypocrites, and I was one of the biggest. I turned my back on God and the things that I learned in church and committed my life to being the best athlete and particularly the best football player I could be. In 1978, my junior year in high school, I became a blue-chip All-American. I was considered to be one of the best athletes in the country. I had letters, scholarship offers from every major university in the nation. There were newspaper articles and clippings. My god, athletics, had come through. I was on top of the world, or so I thought.

Sometimes God Has To Break You To Make You

At the beginning of the football season in 1979, I was predicted to be "the man of Woodrow Wilson." All the colleges were waiting, and my future looked bright! I caught three touchdowns our first game, intercepted four passes, made 17 tackles, and sacked the quarterback twice. The headlines read: "Johnson Unstoppable"!

In our first district high school football game, the second game of the season I was thinking, "I'm the man. I'm mean. I'm bad. I'm agile." I was mostly hostile and highly motivated. I had believed the hype of the newspapers. On the first play of the game, I scored a touchdown. In the first half, I made 10 tackles, intercepted one pass, and I was having a great game. I never left the field, I played wide receiver on offense and on defense, strong safety. I was on kick off and kick off return and punt and punt return. Then a funny thing happened. It's funny how life can change in a matter of seconds. The other team was punting the ball after we stopped them defensively, and as I went in to block a punt, diving in the air, someone upended me and I landed on my head. I was stunned and shaken, but I managed to get to my feet and make a block. We huddled, and the very next play a big running back received a pitch out. At that point, as I replay what happened next, it was as if life began to go in slow motion. Like hundreds of other times, I lowered my head and attempted to make the tackle. The top of my helmet hit the runner on the outer portion of his thigh and my entire body felt as if it had suddenly caught on fire. I made the tackle and I fell on my back, motionless. Coaches ran onto the field, and for a few minutes, I couldn't move. I tried to get up, but my whole body wouldn't respond. By this time, my mom, my step dad, Big Lou, and friends were on the field too. As they attempted to move me, I regained the feeling in my arms and legs and I jumped to my feet. On the sidelines, I was able to run and jump, but when I attempted to put my helmet on my neck, my back felt as if it were on fire again and I lost feeling in my hands. They rushed me to the hospital while still in my uniform, x-rays were taken, and it was discovered that I had cracked the 5th vertebrae in my neck. My god, football, was taken in a matter of seconds.

The next day, I lay in the hospital bed with some type of object pulling my head away from my body, separating my spinal column. I couldn't move. In fact, I was motionless from my neck down for two weeks. As I lay there, I cursed God but tried to maintain a positive demeanor for the visitors who came by to see me. There were newspaper articles with headlines that read: "Blue-Chip Falls Due To Paralyzing Neck Injury." Sometimes God has to break you to make you, and as I lay in that bed, I played the "let's make a deal" game with God: "If you get me out of this one, I promise I'll never turn my back on you again." You ever prayed that prayer?

After those two weeks, the doctors said that they would put me in a halo brace, and boy did I learn what hell feels like. They screwed bolts through the skin of my head and fastened the brace to my skull to prevent my head from turning, and they fastened these long rods that hooked to a harness that fastened around my midsection. I had no pain medication and I was awake and conscious during the whole procedure. You want to talk about pain? That procedure hurt! I stayed in the brace for three months and studied through an in-house tutor because I couldn't attend classes due to the danger of being bumped, falling, etc., and I had to keep my head straight. That was an experience! You really find out who your friends are when adversity strikes. I want to thank God for my mom, coaches, family members and friends who supported me during this time in my life.

Let's Make A Deal

One night, some of my friends had come over to try to cheer me up and brought the usual party necessities. We were outside getting high and some street witnesses came up and began ministering to us. They saw me looking like Frankenstein and began to speak truth. Some of my friends began to mock them, stating that there is no God and that these people were stupid and wasting their time talking to us. One of the men looked at me and said, "Do you remember the deal you made with God?" I tried to look away as if I didn't know what he was talking about, but deep down inside I remembered that prayer. They asked permission to pray for me. I agreed and they walked away. Then I got this unusual sickening feeling in the pit of my stomach and told my friends that they had to leave because I wasn't feeling well.

It was late in the evening, and I went straight to my bed and began to cry and to ask God to forgive me. And again I prayed that prayer: "I'm sorry, God. Give me one more chance." Over the course of those three months, I'd had several hospital visits so that the doctors could survey whether or not the brace could be removed. After this incident with the witnesses, I had another appointment. On several of my previous visits, the doctors had said that they would remove the brace on the next visit, but sadly, each time they would tell me again that it wasn't ready to be removed. It was very awkward being in this brace. I had to sleep straight up on my back with pillows elevating my head. Trying to take baths and not get the cloth portion of the brace wet and cutting some of my shirts to get dressed was very unpleasant.

So this visit I prayed to God to let this be the time I got out of this thing, and I promised that I would do what the witnesses talked about. And then it happened: I was free! At the doctor's office, they took that brace off, and being too cool for school, I was back! Bird was back!! I put my Bible back on the shelf and athletics and being cool took front and center stage again. I made a comeback in track because I wasn't allowed to play basketball, and that year I won the district in the 440 yard dash with the best time in the state. I received many honors and made it to the state championships where I got second. The scholarship offers began to come in again, and after six visits to different universities in 1979, I signed a letter of intent to attend the University of Tulsa to play football. I didn't totally turn my back on God, however. No matter how far in the world I seemed to get, I always went to church because I had this in the back of my mind: Don't mess with God or He will get you. Not the right state of mind, but at least not out of bounds.

CHAPTER FIVE

College:

The Crossroads

"This is what the Lord says: 'Stand at the crossroads and look; ask for the ancient paths, ask where the good way is, and walk in it, and you will find rest for your souls.'"

Jeremiah 6:16

The four and one-half hour drive from Dallas, Texas to Tulsa, Oklahoma seemed like a lifetime. Big Lou drove to Tulsa with me and a good friend, Vince Murray, to deliver us and all of our belongings. Once at Tulsa University, we went straight to the Athletic Dorm (Jock Dorm), and I can still smell the fresh paint and the old tennis shoes, hear the music coming from different rooms, and see the coaches as they greeted us and our dorm mother who gave us our keys and assigned our room. Vince was my roommate, and we were now student athletes.

Big Lou gave us hugs and began his journey back to Dallas, and after unpacking most of our stuff, Vince and I went to the athletic office for our first team meeting with all the other incoming freshman. We received our counselors and information on how to get registered for classes and all the rules and regulations and expectations for us as freshman.

The next day, we had a serious workout. They also tested us on different agility moves and timed us, weighed us, prodded us, measured us and anything else they could think of to determine our value as football players. We practiced for one week before the upperclassmen arrived. In the cafeteria, the upperclassmen made the freshman sing the school fight song standing on the tables and carrying their trays after they were finished eating. When guys as big as trucks tell you what to do, believe me, you don't give much argument or disapproval. But I was not the average kind of guy. I rebelled, because I was too cool to be anybody's boy, and boy did I pay the price! The first day of practice with the upperclassmen was ten times intensified and intimidating. These guys brought intensity, enthusiasm and effort to another level. Two-a-day practices had begun, and I discovered muscles I never knew I had by the pain located in them. The coaches broke us down to build us up again.

Classes hadn't begun yet, and I thought college was a piece of cake—until the first day of class. A typical day: up at 6:00 a.m. for breakfast, then to the first class at 8:00 a.m., and go to classes until 11:00 a.m.. Lunch at noon, classes from 1:00 p.m. to 3:00 p.m. Then getting taped for football practice by 3:30 p.m., practice from 4:00 - 6:30 p.m., or until the coaches felt we were finished, dinner generally from 6:30 - 8:00 p.m., team meetings and watching film from 8:30 - 10:00 p.m. Then there was mandatory study hall from 10:00-11:00 p.m., and only after all that did you have any time to study beyond this one hour a day or for a personal life.

I Broke the Deal

My freshman and sophomore year is sketchy in my memory. I didn't play or make any traveling teams. I spent most of my time on the scout team and in a haze of just trying to fit in, be cool, stay high and conquer as many women as I could. To say the least, I was a fool. For me at this time in my life, God was no more than something I did on Sunday to show that I wasn't a total heathen. I was very bitter, not playing football, and the drugs I used were destroying my capacity to think or feel. I was also trying to live up to this sugar hill image I had created to try to be the pimp daddy on campus. I discovered male dancing and began to make money. Football and college were part of the game that I was using to try and present myself as this whole-some, all American boy, who had come out of the ghetto to try to find a place in this world. I was still *stuck on stupid.*

An example of this was, during times of reckless liv-ing and dancing, one night of partying and premarital sex led to more than I bargained for. I slept with a young lady and I found out a month later that she was pregnant. A part of me wanted to deny it and a part of me knew it could be mine. So at the hospital eight months later, Kenneth Dominick Johnson was born, and I took the responsibility of supporting him the best I could.

Racism became a very prevalent part of my life because I saw many white athletes given what I thought was special treatment from coaches, and many black athletes like myself were continually humiliated and had to do twice as much to be considered equal. Past memories of how whites used to treat us when they would come to our neighborhoods during Christmas and hand out hand-me-down toys and soiled clothing began to haunt me. How they would give us hot dogs, chips and watered down Kool-Aid and tell us how much Jesus loved us, and then we would never see them again.

There was one group in college I hated, the Fellowship of Christian Athletes (FCA). There were no blacks involved, and the athletes involved were a group of men who reminded me consistently of who I really was—and I didn't like that. I did not like being reminded that I was a sinner who had no standards, that I had turned by back on the very God who had given me the opportunity to make it to college and to get out of those terrible situations I had been in most of my life.

These guys were very different, so I decided that I would test their commitment, the reality of what they said as they lived it or failed to live it. So, I took any opportunity I had to persecute them, calling them racist names and disturbing their meetings, tormenting the group for their religious stand or anything else I could think of that would make them look bad and put myself in a better light. It had gotten so bad that, if they saw me coming, they would turn and go the opposite way to avoid any confrontation.

There was one guy, however, who always had an encouraging word for me no matter what I did. His name was Skip Ast, a young Christian quarterback who didn't play, and he had the best attitude of anyone I have ever met in similar circumstances. He would always say, "Bird, why do you act so bad, man? You're not as bad as you think you are. I know there's a good man inside you. I see you going to church every Sunday." He was the only white player who ever had anything positive to say to me.

There was also another upperclassman on our team

named Alvin Simpkins whose father was a black minister, and he took it upon himself to confront me, perhaps because he saw something in me that he thought was salvageable. Every Sunday, no matter how late I stayed out or what I had done, he would come by to take me to church. Every Sunday for one year he came to my room and I said no, until one Sunday. I knew he was coming and I got ready. He yelled out, "Bird, are you going to church?" I said, "Yes," thinking he would be shocked, but all he said was, "I'll be downstairs waiting on you." Every Sunday from that point on I went to church with him.

The God of a Second, Third and Fourth Chance

By my junior year, my coaches and teammates had pretty much labeled me gifted and talented but unsalvageable. I was on academic probation and had a .001 grade average. So, the summer before entering my junior year, I was informed that I would need to bring my grades up to a 2.0 by the beginning of the upcoming year or I would not be allowed to return. The coach also informed me that a number of other coaches felt that even if I brought my grades up they did not want me to return. And to top all of this off, I had not talked with my mom since my senior year in high school.

I was involved in ROTC, thinking it would be good for my conditioning and to receive the monthly salary added as an incentive to join. I was also receiving social security from my deceased father. A week before I was scheduled to attend Army Officers' Basic Training camp in Ft. Riley, Kansas, I met a young lady named Della Sanders. I was previously introduced to her about three months prior to this night. We were in a nightclub, sitting with a mutual friend, Maeanna Lightner, and another man. I thought to myself, "Why is a nice looking young lady sitting with such an ugly guy." I was young and arrogant, but these two did not appear to be compatible. I remember thinking to myself that he had to be paying, putting out some serious cash to have her! And with the attitude I had at the time, I wasn't paying for nothing, but she looked as if she wanted me to sit down. Her friend was motioning me to sit down too, but this guy looked at me like I was not welcome and should leave. Being the kind of brother that does not intrude on others' territory, I left; but later I found out that they were not together and she really wanted to meet me.

I saw Della again in the same night club the week before I was scheduled to leave, but this time she was sitting with Maeanna and eight other women. Della and her friends saw me dancing, and after returning to my seat, our mutual friend came to inform me that Della wanted to meet me. I responded, "Half the women in this club want to meet me and I don't have time for games." What an ego! She really expressed the desire that Della had to meet me. I didn't immediately respond until I finished another dance and was leaving the dance floor. As I passed their table, I heard the all ten women say, "CHICKEN!" I responded by pulling a chair up next to Della and beginning a conversation, and the rest is history! We really hit it off and made preparations to communicate. We talked briefly that night after going home. The next day, I called her at work and we made plans to go out to dinner and a movie that evening. We saw each other everyday for the next week, and I brought all of my belongings to her to keep for me while I attended camp.

I had met many ladies prior to meeting Della, but none of them had the impact on me that she did. She was very intelligent as well as a beautiful person. She had a kind heart and these eyes that pierced my soul touched my heart. She really seemed like a person who was very genuine and real. She made me want to be a better man.

I left for camp and Della wrote me three letters a day for six weeks. We corresponded and talked about having a future together. In her letters she gave me a real sense of what a good woman was really about. God used her and those letters to really begin a transformation in my heart and in my mind.

Which Road Are You Gonna Travel?

During the time at camp my mind began to clear up from all the drugs, and from being in an environment that truly challenged me to be a leader through the example that I set. I couldn't rely on being cool. I couldn't be the ladies man. I couldn't get high because of drug testing, and I couldn't use profanity. I had to grow up.

They paired me with a skinny white boy named Bob Owens, a sold out, born-again Christian. He was extremely brilliant but couldn't do one push up, and I was a physical specimen but totally brain dead. What a match! God knew exactly what he was doing. Bob literally loved the hell right out of me. No matter how I tried to hate and persecute him, he would just love me. He would leave encouraging notes, a different gospel pamphlet every night on my bed, and I would hear him praying for me every morning and evening that God would touch my heart and make me the man of God that I could truly be. This man modeled true unconditional love and Christianity.

Combined with Bob, Della's letters, and my mind clearing up, I got involved with Officers Christian Fellowship (OCF), who provided good meals at every meeting. At these meetings I began to hear the truth in a way I had never heard it before, and the experience really began to change me. I wrote letters to Della, telling her how God was doing work in my life and how I looked forward to coming home to be a man of God for her and my teammates; the man that God was calling me to be. But Satan never gives up.

One evening, on my way to one of the OCF meetings, I had about fifteen minutes to kill. It was the first time in my life, since meeting Della, that I had not done any drugs and had not been sexually active, and I was feeling pretty good about myself and what God was doing with me. As I walked through this park, I noticed a young man with an infant seat on top of his car. He had a cooler sitting next to the seat, so I walked up to take a look at the baby and got into a conversation. I found out that he was from Dallas and that we had many mutual friends from the same old stomping grounds. By this time, I had ten minutes before the meeting started. He offered me a beer. I had a Bible in my hand, and I declined. He asked what I was doing, and I told him the building number where the OCF meetings were held. He told me that he was going right by this building on his way somewhere else so he would give me a ride. Once inside the car, he fired up a joint and tried to pass it to me. I declined once again because of the Bible in my hand. I couldn't put the Bible on the floor, and I couldn't put it next to me on the seat because of the cooler, so I put it on my lap. He asked if I was a Christian, and I told him I was searching for the truth in my life.

By this time, we arrived at our destination and had five minutes before the start of the meeting. As I stepped out of the car and he took the baby into the apartment building, two young ladies came out with him and asked me to come in; they were very attractive. As I turned around to put the Bible in the car, I looked over at the building where the OCF meeting was to be held, and six guys were standing out front with their Bibles. It is as if God was asking me, "What do you want to do? You are at a crossroads in your life, and you know where the life you've been leading will take you, so why not try me?" I pulled the Bible out of the car and told the young man and the ladies that my meeting was about to begin, that I would see them later. I walked over to the six men who were to attend the meeting and made the number of completion, seven! That meeting was the best Bible study I have ever been involved with, and that day I rededicated my life to Christ after telling the story of what just happened to me and began a new journey in July 1982—a journey, truly, toward excellence.

CHAPTER SIX

Another Second Chance: Our New Family Begins

"A wife of noble character who can find? She is worth far more than rubies. Her husband has full confidence in her and lacks nothing of value. She brings him good, not harm, all the days of her life."

Proverbs 31:10-12

The first day I got home from military camp, I put a ring on Della's finger and asked her to marry me. She accepted. She had been married before, in a very abusive and adulterous relationship, and was somewhat apprehensive, but she could see the change in me and what God was doing in my life. The football team, on the other hand, the coaches and Christian athletes and party brothers were not so convinced. The coaches thought I was trying to pull some emotional plea, the Christians thought it was a trick, and my party brothers thought I was going crazy. But Della was right there and so was Skip.

One day in the weight room, I was talking about what God was doing in my life and some of the Christian players were telling me God can do anything, but even God couldn't change Bird. They remembered the old Bird. Skip, on the other hand, told me that if I was serious, to go and look up II Corinthians 5:17: "Therefore, if any man be in Christ, he is a new creature: old things are passed away; behold, all things are become new" (KJV). When I read that scripture, all the questions and all the statements being made about me didn't matter anymore.

Whenever someone would ask me what made me think that I could change, whenever they would ask me why they should trust me now, all I would have to say is: Therefore, if any man be in Christ, he is a NEW creature! God has made me new. It took some time, but slowly and surely living according to biblical scriptures and letting my walking do my talking, people began to see that God had truly touched me. James 2: 17: "In the same way, faith by itself, if it is not accompanied by action, is dead". My faith moved from being something that I did to being something that I lived. Della was the first lady that didn't put up with any of my stuff and helped me evaluate all the people in my life. She helped me through that woman's intuition they all have. She helped me study, made me read, and typed my term papers to raise my grade point. That one year alone my GPA went from a .001 to a 2.5.

Family First

One situation that sticks out to me, and one of the con-
firmations that let me know that Della was right for me, was
her strong stand on family. Della's mother had passed approximately two years before I met her; she died of Lou Gehrig's
disease. Her mother had a deep impact on her life, and she knew
about my situation and prodded me (prodded in her presence
and nagged me in her absence) to call my mother to mend that
relationship. I explained that I had vowed to never speak to my
mom again, and at that time it had been over two years. Let it
suffice to say that it wasn't a pleasant situation the summer I left
home to go to college. This was Mother's Day 1982 and Della
was consistently bugging me to call my mom. So, to get some
peace I called Mom; and the first thing that she said was, "Um, I
thought you were dead," in a very sarcastic tone of voice. I was
about to hang up the phone when Della grabbed the receiver and
told me to keep talking. I told Mom I had met someone and we
were getting married and she wanted to meet her. Mom started to
cry and apologized, and I put Della on the phone. We still do that
today. Della is the communicator to all of our family members
with any and everything that concerns the family.

Eight months later, in February 1983, one of the happi-
est days of my life occurred: Della and I were married. Yes, we
moved fast! When you know, you know! That same year I had
a knee injury that enabled me to receive a red-shirt, which gave
me an extra year of eligibility. What I thought were lemons, God
gave me in order to make lemonade. With that extra year, I was
able to catch up on much needed classes, went to summer class,
and all in all did really well. That summer I had a 4.0 in all the
classes I took. That year I was injured I spent all my extra time
in the weight room, and consequently, I went from 225 lbs. to
400 lbs. on the bench, 300-600 lbs. on my squats, and my dead

lift went from 300-600 lbs. and my power clean from 225 to over 350 lbs. My 40 time also went from 4.6 to 4.3 seconds, and I gained weight naturally, without steroids, all this advancement through clean living and good love. I became the strongest and fastest defensive back on the team. After returning from the injury, I started as strong safety and became captain of special teams. Also, I was the strongest man on my team for my size.

God really blessed me to become a positive influence on the team. I even led a Bible study for some of the young players and was the only African American involved in the FCA organization's weekly meetings. Eventually, I helped bring many more African Americans to the meetings, however. After practice one day, I was singing a song I loved, "Reasons" by Earth, Wind and Fire, and one of the players and FCA leaders, Kevin Harlan, heard me singing and asked if I would sing in one of the FCA meetings. I didn't have any Christian songs, so Kevin went out and purchased my first soundtrack, "The Sky is the Limit" by Leon Patillo. We spent an hour going over it to make sure I sang it correctly because I had never sung to a track before. I laugh about it now, thinking about this white boy teaching me the right way to sing! I still sing it today! By the end of my senior year I was starting at strong safety, raised my grade point average to a 3.5, and Della and I were doing great as newlyweds. I got involved in a Bible study led by Bill Blankenship, where I was discipled through that FCA group. I learned about quiet time and scripture memorization, and for the first time sensed a call to preach the gospel. I had begun to speak and share my testimony through FCA, and this began to seem like a prelude to something larger.

Life was good! I was even getting looks from professional football scouts and thought about playing. It's always a dream to an inner city kid to do good and make money to help his family, but the second to the last game of the season that knee injury snapped one day in practice and any hopes of continuing a football career were gone. But I still had God and I was still going to graduate. I was commissioned as a 2nd Lieutenant in the U.S. Army, and even though I wasn't real sure of what I was going to do for a career, I had total peace that God was in complete control of my life. In 1984, I was the first member of my family to graduate from college, and I did it with a 3.5 grade point and the help and the love of a good wife and a mighty God.

All things work together for the good. I stated earlier in 1980 I had a son out of wedlock with my family, my hope and prayer is to live, love, learn and leave a legacy. I will talk a lot about Kendall and Kristina but what about my oldest son Kenneth Dominick? After many years of fathering from afar, long distance parenting has not been the ideal situation. But God has really blessed our relationship. Almost every Christmas, birthday and summer he has spent with me and the family. Della considered him a son and Kendall and Kristina truly know him as brother. In 1994 he excepted Christ as his personal savior at an Fellowship of Christian Athletes camp at Black Mountain, North Carolina.

Satin has always tried to tell me that because I had a son and I was not married I could not be used for God's good because I was a hypocrite to encourage children to stay sexually pure before marriage when I didn't do it myself. But Gods word tells me that his grace is sufficient for me and that through my painful experience I can help other children not make some of the same mistakes I made to save them from that pain. Today Dominick is living in Tulsa and doing very well. You may have had something in your life happen that Satin is trying to use against you to disqualify you from God's work. All you have to do is repent, turn from your wicked ways and ask God to forgive you. I am a witness God can work out for the good what the devil meant for bad.

If God can rescue the eagle from the chicken coop, and get me off being *stuck on stupid*, doesn't it make sense He can do the same for you and use you in a mighty way to further His kingdom?

CHAPTER SEVEN

Blood on a Badge:

God Can Use You Where You Are

"But let all who take refuge in you be glad; let them ever sing for joy. Spread your protection over them, that those who love your name may rejoice in you."

Psalm 5:11

After college, pro football didn't become a reality, so I had to get a real job. I toyed with the idea of going full-time active duty in the military or working odd jobs. I thought of becoming a personal fitness trainer or working for a van lines company. I thought about becoming a youth pastor for a church or working with the Fellowship of Christian Athletes. Della and I were going into our second year of marriage. She had a promising career with an oil company, and I needed to find something that would enable me to take care of her and our future family.

An opportunity dropped into my lap that I had not anticipated. A friend and fellow reservist mentioned that the Tulsa Police Academy was recruiting minorities and suggested I apply. I told him he was crazy, out of his mind. There was no way I would be a police officer. As they say, "Never say never!" I learned later that he had entered my name along with his to the recruiter. About a week later, I received a call from the recruiter for the police department and we scheduled an interview. It's amazing how God will set you up! I talked to Della about this opportunity, and she was dead set against it. She had the typical reservations about the job that most women do.

After praying about it, I thought, "What could I lose?" Maybe it was my sense of curiosity or the timing of events, but this opportunity was something tangible that would provide security for myself and my family. Reluctantly, I kept the appointment. I dressed very casually, hoping that I would not make an impression. I wore an FCA t-shirt, jeans and tennis shoes. As soon as I walked into the office, I was met by a 5'5", 170 lb. recruiting officer. As he looked up at me, smiling at my biceps, I felt as though I were being sized up for battle! The first words out of his mouth were, "My God, how much do you lift?"

After a brief introduction, he handed me a test and stated that he didn't think I would have any problems. He told me, however, that the class was starting in one week and that I would probably have to wait for the next class scheduled to begin in four months. After taking the test, he graded it immediately and asked if I could be back the next day for the physical fitness test. This was Thursday. I returned Friday morning, prepared for the physical fitness test. I maxed the test and recorded the best time ever. Needless to say, this was more than impressive.

I was asked to return that same evening for an oral board review. An oral board is a group of men who ask hypothetical questions about how you would handle certain situations. All I did in the oral session was preach the gospel. After this portion, I was asked to wait in a room for my results. After thirty minutes, the recruiter informed me that there is generally a 3-4 month background investigation before placement is made for a cadet into the academy, but if I was willing to start the academy the upcoming Monday, the investigation would be completed by the end of my training. I would start immediately. Three months later, I graduated from the Tulsa Police Academy, the same day my background investigation was completed, and I passed with flying colors! It's amazing how God works.

My first day on the street, I prayed, "God, may your blood cover my badge and cover my life, and may everything I do be a shining example of how good your love is." For the next six years I worked as an officer, and I recall praying that prayer several times. My experience as a police officer prepared and equipped me more than any area of my life for the ministry. Also, the four year licensing and ordination process through Higher Dimension Family Center in Tulsa gave me the spiritual and organizational structure to understand my call.

All the college courses, military training, and even the hundreds of times I had spoken at FCA functions and other ministry gatherings, did not compare with seeing Satan at his best. As a police officer, you see the worst of the worst: what people can do, and what they actually do, to one another. You see babies molested, wives and husbands in continual turmoil, people ravaged by destructive behavior, homes destroyed by alcohol and drug abuse. Almost every day of your life, you are bombarded with the destructive forces of the devil, with how he twists and deceives every facet of human existence. I learned who the devil really was and how to recognize what he does to kill, steal, and destroy.

As an officer you have many stories to tell, but here are a couple if incidents that stand out:

The Male Streaker

I had been on the job for about four years, and everybody in the community I patrolled knew me. I also worked as a security guard at one of the high schools in that community and ran a FCA huddle group during the evening. As I was patrolling the neighborhood around the school, I saw a large gathering of youth and other individuals walking down the middle of the street as if there were a fight or some other event the crowd desperately wanted to see. I can remember coming to a stop and giving the dispatcher my location and getting out of my car to investigate what was going on. I turned on my overhead lights and the crowd began to move toward my car as if Moses had parted the red sea. And then, out from the crowd came a man with only his shoes and socks on. Needless to say, this was not what I expected. He spotted my car and headed straight for it. When he got close enough, I grabbed his arm and leaned him against the car, but he jumped on the hood and began to do some exotic dancing.

All the people following this event now had surrounded the car, so I grabbed his ankles and pulled him down. He landed on his ribs and I could smell the PCP and marijuana on him. PCP smells like lighter fluid and fingernail polish mixed together. It gives you superhuman strength and makes you oblivious to pain. As I attempted to handcuff this young man, he began to fight, and between the blood that was now coming from his nose, the sweat coming from his body and the gerry curl juice coming from his hair, he had become a slippery mess and I could not subdue him. I had to sit on him until my backup arrived, at which time we handcuffed him. But we were still unable to put this 5'9", 170lb man in the car because he was so high on the PCP. The more we tried to put him in my car, the more abusive he became to himself. So we had to call an ambulance to have him sandwiched in the gurneys and transported to the hospital for his injuries and eventually to jail. This stands out because the drug PCP became the drug of choice at that time, and it was the first of many calls where people would unclothe and do unthinkable things to themselves and others.

Preacher

I got my street name, Preacher, from some gang members who were students at the high school where I ran the FCA huddle. It had been common knowledge that I was a minister and that if I arrested you that I would attempt to lead you to Christ on my way to lockup. One of the young men who had been arrested for possession of firearms and commission of a felony tells a story to some of his friends about how, on his way to jail, I pulled my police car over in an alley and began to preach to him for about thirty minutes. He did accept the Lord and prayed that God would get him out of the situation he was in. He was saved and got involved with my FCA group, joined the football team, got out of the gang and went to college. He and a few others nicknamed me Preacher and the name stuck. Now he works as a Tulsa Police officer in the inner-city where I used to patrol. Truly, God's blood was on the badge.

Woman, Put Some Clothes On

The divorce rate among police officers is one of the highest in the nation among all professions. One of the reasons is the flexible hours and the number of strangers and individuals you run into on a daily basis. Some people say men in uniform are very attractive, but it could also be the tremendous amount of power you have as a police officer that attracts people. Whatever the case may be, I continually found myself being propositioned and flirted with as an officer. As a married Christian and minister, I felt my responsibility was to set an example in the area of sexual purity. Ninety percent of the guys in my squad had divorced due to marital unfaithfulness, and I was always counseling guys in the area of marital and integrity issues.

On one particular day, I received a call to take a burglary report. As I went to the home, as I had done a number of times, I was met by the victim, who stated that her home had been burglarized and gave me a list of all the things taken. I could see that the house had been ransacked and the back door had been kicked in, destroying the lock and hinges. I made the report, listed the items, and like many other times, I told the victim that if she found any other items before I got off my shift to give me a call and I would come back to add them to the report so that she wouldn't have to make an additional report.

The woman was very attractive and stated that she was a model. She was also somewhat flirtatious with me. I was always courteous but endeavored not to lead anyone to the wrong conclusion about my motives. I thought nothing of it and went on my way. About an hour later, I received a call from dispatch to return to the same address to receive more information about items that were taken. When I approached the door of the residence, I could see that it was open. As I rang the doorbell, I could hear someone inside the home scream, "Just come in. I'm getting out of the shower." Her response gave me an instant check in my spirit and something said, don't go in the house, so I pushed the door open and the woman came out of her bedroom with a towel wrapped around her that conveniently dropped to the floor as she tried to flip her hair out of the way. From the depths of my soul, someone said, "Woman, put some clothes on." I know it had to be the Holy Spirit, because truly, a part of me could not help but notice that she looked nice. She really was inviting, but the spirit man in me would not allow me to place myself in a situation of compromise. I was able to witness to the young lady and made what could have been a very bad situation into something that I feel truly gave glory to God. The first thing I did when I got home was tell my wife what happened, and we both laughed and praised God. I tell men all the time that, when they are confronted with those Jezebel's, they must be like Joseph—RUUUUNNNNNN! Truly, God's blood was on the badge.

All We have to do is Pray

I was called to a domestic disturbance where the man (as in many other cases) had physically assaulted his wife, and it was a very heated and bloody scene. Kids were downstairs screaming, and the father had barricaded himself upstairs with the mother, threatening to kill her. As our supervisor and other officers arrived, the situation grew more and more intense. We removed the children from the home, and our sergeant asked, "What next?" And the only thing I could say was, "Let's pray."

The man holding his wife hostage did not know that I was the officer downstairs and stated to my sergeant that he wouldn't come out unless the officer named Preacher came to the scene. My sergeant informed him that I was on the scene. As I began to talk with the man, the first thing I told him was that we needed to pray about how we should handle the situation. I told him that he should pray with me about what God wanted him to do in this instance. Immediately after the prayer, he let his wife go and gave her the gun. Shortly thereafter, he came down himself and was taken into custody. He later received counseling and I personally followed up with him and his wife. I also assisted him in getting a job and getting involved in one of the local churches in the area. Truly, God's blood was on the badge.

Family and the Church

All the counselors say that, when you become a police officer, over a period of time you begin to change, your heart becomes hard from all the negative things you see constantly. I had been on the job for two years, my oldest son Kenneth Dominick was four years old; my son, Kendall, was born; and then fourteen months later, my little girl, Kristina, came along. Della began to first notice the change in me and how callous and short tempered my attitude was becoming. She would make little comments as her way of encouraging me to spend more time with her and the kids. My world revolved around work, church, work, church, work, church and family. Even though I had the Lord in my heart and lived 100% for Him, even though the blood was covering my badge, I didn't allow it to cover my family and Satan began to creep in. I thought that by providing the physical necessities, such as a house, clothes, food, a car, things, I was doing what God called me to do. I was speaking in the community and being very civic- and community-oriented, but I seemed to have time for everybody but my family. After constant prodding when I'd come home, Della left me, which was a wakeup call for me; a time to examine what was really important.

Wake Up Call

I went to church that night, and a man named Ed Cole was the speaker. This was long before Promise Keepers evolved.

I was an elder at Higher Dimensions, and I had maintained the appearance that my life and family were all together. I didn't know where Della was, and when asked where she was, I told people she was at home because she was not feeling well. You ever lied in church? I did, and as a man of God. It's amazing what we'll do to keep that holy face on.

As Ed Cole began to speak, I felt as though Della had slipped a note to him about my life and he was speaking directly to me. As he talked about a man who had time for everyone in the ministry but not for his family, a man who didn't pray or be the priest of his home, a man who was not maximized to be God's man, this speaker ripped me to shreds that night. And when he gave the alter call, I was the first one to the altar asking God to forgive me and to make me this maximized man he was talking about. I bought every book, tape and piece of merchandise he had, and as I drove home, I prayed that God would send my wife and babies back. Sometimes God will give you a wake up call to let you know what's really important in life.

Della had gone to her grandmother's house, Mother Stephens, who told her to simply love her husband anyhow. She told her that I was a good man and just confused, to let God change me and work on her. I called her the next day at work and asked her to come home so that we could talk, and I told her what God had laid on my heart for us. She came, and God began the process to put our marriage truly back together. That is when I made the commitment to come home and do whatever it took to be God's maximized man for my wife, sons, and little baby girl. There have been hills and valleys, and it hasn't always been easy, but the past years have been a commitment to keep God's blood over our lives in everything that we do not just on the badge. TO GOD BE THE GLORY!

As a police officer you spend the majority of your time in a reactionary mode. As a minister, the child of a King, I was constantly looking for opportunities to be proactive verses reactive.

I became the first black person, and youngest person overall, to ever become elected to Police for Christ, a two hundred and fifty member organization that spreads the love of Jesus to police officers. I became the Chaplain of the Black Officers Coalition, and I started an organization called SHARE (Stand, Help, And Rid Evil), which assisted in the needs of inner-city inhabitants by passing out fans to the elderly, Thanksgiving food baskets, and holding toy drives for children during Christmas. I also helped coordinate with local churches to assist families with counseling on an on-going basis, with housing assistance, job placement and any other need they had in their lives.

Over a period of time, it became very obvious that God wanted me to go into full-time service for Him. In June 1990, after selling our home, we left $70,000 a year jobs, took our two children and moved to Indianapolis, Indiana to work for the Fellowship of Christian Athletes for less than half the salary of our previous yearly income. And God still made a way!

CHAPTER EIGHT

The Ministry, the Work:

The Call of God

"But you, keep your head in all situations, endure hardship, do the work of an evangelist, discharge all the duties of your ministry."

2 Timothy 4:5

Leaving the police department was not an easy decision. But through the many situations that occurred while a police officer, I knew for certain that God was calling me into full-time ministry. I was always in conflict with my supervisors and with some individuals in the community who frowned upon my open ministry as an officer. Many people thought that ministry had no place in the police department, and much of the attention I was getting in the media was making me controversial.

One instance that confirmed that God was calling me out of the police department was when we had started a foot patrol unit that got us out of the cars and into walking around into some of the apartment complexes in the inner city. We were trying to get back a feeling of trust by letting the people in the community know us on a personal level. We were very successful, and because of our efforts, many churches and community leaders rallied around the success of the program. Christ was being glorified and lives were being changed.

Because some people from the ACLU felt that what I was doing was not a separation of church and state, letters were written and some of those people began to protest. One day, I was working on the behalf of the less fortunate, and the next day I found myself being transferred to a completely different part of town and having new duties and responsibilities assigned to me. The worst part about the situation was that I had no advance warning or written notice of the transfer. The chief and the supervisors just made the decision without consulting me or even giving me an opportunity to conform, or at least to do things a little differently. I was so offended and insulted that I had decided to quit, but after talking and praying with my wife and many community leaders and pastors, we all felt that this was a test from God to see what I really stood for. It was decided that to quit would be to allow the devil to have the victory. The situation was bigger than my personal feelings or ego.

It had gotten back to the chief that I was quitting, however, and many people in the community were upset. They decided that whatever I wanted to do they would do. The department had a meeting, and when I arrived I told them that God had a plan bigger for my life, that whatever they wanted me to do I would comply with. Needless to say, they were shocked. They were anticipating that I would come in with all sorts of demands, but I told them that God was in control. The department transferred me back to a regular patrol unit, and the sergeant, who had heard what had happened, was anticipating that I would have a bad attitude and would cause trouble for his unit. He did not hear about my response to what the department did to me at this point, and when he found out, he was amazed, even somewhat perplexed. I learned later that he was wondering why I hadn't taken the department to court.

I worked for that sergeant for about six months, and even counseled him on many issues that he was dealing with in his personal life. I also received an outstanding evaluation from him on my performance under his command. I was transferred to the academy to work part-time as the physical fitness instructor for the academy classes and was being groomed to be one the recruiters for minority applicants.

During this time, I was invited to sing at the 1989 FCA National Convention in Indianapolis. While in Indianapolis, I had many job offers to work as urban director in different areas around the country; but the Indianapolis offer seemed to be where God was calling me and wanted me to be. I was sold, but I had to sell Della. She had family, friends, a good job, church, doctors, a nice home and a major sense of comfort; but she also knew what I had been through on the police force and wasn't completely closed to the idea of me going into full-time ministry. Her worrying about the danger of the occupation and me coming home in one piece may have played a part in her being open too, and maybe she sensed the call of God on my life. Whatever the reason, she made a deal with God. She prayed that, if he sold our house, this would be her confirmation to move. Keep in mind that a house in our neighborhood had not sold in two years. However, the day after the sale sign went in the yard, the first couple who looked at the house bought it. Do you think it was a confirmation? Three months after the job offer, we resigned from our jobs, sold our house, came to Indianapolis to buy a home, closed on the new home the day our furniture arrived, packed up the kids, said all our good-byes to our loved ones in Tulsa, and started our new life in Indianapolis.

With renewed excitement and enthusiasm, I began as Urban Director of Indiana for FCA. My job was to present to urban athletes and coaches and all they influence the challenge and adventure of receiving Jesus Christ as their personal Lord and Savior, serving him in a relationship and fellowship of the church. I was back working for the same organization with some of the same guys who had discipled me in college: Kevin Harlan, the brother who brought my first sound track; Chad Craig, the big 6'9" offensive lineman who flew planes in his spare time; and many others. I began speaking in schools, singing at banquets, and raising funds to send inner-city youth to camp. I was helping coaches with different needs and seeing hundreds of kids give their lives to a mighty Savior. We had a great team: Glen Korobov, State Director; Carol Long; Rob Kirk; and Shelley Birkholtz. Boy, did we do the work of the Lord.

Pro Football Finally

After being in Indianapolis for two months, I was invited to speak at a Colts chapel service by a former teammate to whom I had introduced Christ at TU, Donnie Dee. He was playing for the Colts at the time. The chaplain of the Colts at that time was Rev. John Rayls, who was with a ministry called "SEARCH." God really used me to speak the word at that service, and many of the African American players who had been encouraged to come by Donnie really bonded with me and asked me to come back and meet with them one on one. The head coach, Ron Meyer, even asked me to consider traveling with the team, but I declined. One week after that meeting, John asked if I would consider replacing him as the Colts' Protestant Chaplain. I prayerfully considered accepting his offer and was overjoyed that God was giving me an opportunity to minister to men we read about and see on television.

Athletes have such a great platform from which to deliver a positive message to almost every area of our society, a platform that could be greatly used to lift up the name of Jesus Christ. Since 1990, God has allowed me to help shape and mold character, to shape the integrity of these men, and to encourage biblical holiness in many athletes who have in turn become not only better athletes but husbands, fathers, and Godly role models for all who look to them as heroes. Also, since I wasn't able to play, it's as if God has allowed me to be a part of professional athletics. I did make it to the pros. Not the way I thought I would, but I made it!

A group that has been of assistance in accomplishing what God has given me to do with the Colts is PAO (Pro Athletes Outreach), which is directed by Norm and Barb Evans. Norm is a former Miami Dolphin and helps all NFL team chaplains coordinate and communicate with one another. PAO also holds a yearly conference that addresses the needs of the athlete. In 1993, Della and I attended our first PAO conference, and it helped strengthen and solidify our marriage and our love for one another and our children. We attend the conference every year and wouldn't miss it for the world. We thank God for Norm and Barb and for the work they do. They are impacting hundreds of athletes all over the country. We encourage many athletes from the team to attend, and we've seen marriages that seemed to be on the verge of ending come back together and get straightened out. These are couples like ourselves who just need to fall deeper in love with each other, and there was even a couple from our team who came as singles and left married.

We've seen our chapel attendance grow from two to over fifty guys on a regular basis and our Bible study grew from two to over twenty five. Della has been working with as many as fifteen of the wives, and we've been able to lead young players to the Lord, and to in turn utilize many of them to assist us in speaking for the Lord in many different areas in the community. No matter how good God is and what he's calling you to do, He always wants you to do a little bit more. He wants you out of the coop and soaring. It's your choice to choose how high you want to fly.

CHAPTER NINE

Peer Pressure: The Power to Conform

"Therefore I urge you brother, in view of God's mercy, to offer your bodies as a living sacrifice, Holy and pleasing to God. This is your spiritual act of worship. Do not conform any longer to the pattern of this world, but be transformed by the renewing of your mind. Then you will be able to test and approve what God's will is - his good, pleasing and perfect will."

Romans 12:1-2

Not only do we need to renew the minds of kids, but adults as well. Often when we talk about peer pressure, it's in the negative perspective. We also have to realize that peer pressure can be viewed from a positive perspective. In the Chicken Eagle story, for example, the little eagle was pressured to conform to the standards of the coop by the mother hen and chickens. The preceeding scripture tells us not to conform to the patterns of this world, but to be transformed by the renewing of our mind. I like to call it not being *stuck on stupid*. Proverbs 12:1 says, "Whoever loves discipline loves knowledge, but whoever hates correction is stupid." So, if someone is trying to give you knowledge that will help create discipline in your life, that will prevent you from making costly mistakes, but if you have the attitude that no one can tell you anything or correct you, then you are *stuck on stupid*.

In 1991 I was "Mean Dean" at an FCA junior high boys sports camp in Black Mountain, North Carolina. I was in charge of discipline making sure all the boys had a healthy respect for the rules and expectation of the camp. One of my responsibilities was making announcements every evening of how the campers were conducting themselves and to make correction on any behavior that would be detrimental to the camp or the campers. It had come to my attention that many of the campers were jumping from building to building. The buildings were over four stories tall and two feet apart. I strongly rebuked and told the boys to stop this crazy practice because someone could get hurt. As you can guess that very evening before lights out a young man while attempting the mighty leap didn't make it and plunged four stories, breaking both legs and fracturing an arm and puncturing a lung and having to be rushed to the emergency room. The next morning in my quiet time I just happened to be reading Proverbs 12:1-2. For the morning announcements this scripture was fresh on my mind. I told the boys, not listening to sound advice led to one of their campers being severely hurt and I asked the question, "are you going to stay *stuck on stupid* for the remaining of camp by not listening to all that God is speaking through the people he has sent here to help you?" The term *stuck on stupid* became the camp theme for the week. The huddle made up banners, signs and t-shirts and I've been using the term since then.

It's what you have learned after you thought you know it all that counts. "All scripture is God breathed and is useful for teaching, rebuking, correcting and training in righteousness, so that the man of God may be thoroughly equipped for every good work" (2 Timothy 3:16). Jesus said, "Enter through the narrow gate. For wide is the gate and broad is the road that leads to destruction, and many enter through it. But small is the gate and narrow the road that leads to life, and only a few find it" (Matthew 7:13-14). The devil is using the things of this world to set a huge trap for those who get *stuck on stupid*. After chasing the things of this world trying to get ahead, all they really get is a lot of pain, discouragement, disappointment and eventually death.

Some classic examples of being *stuck on stupid* include:

- Being strung out on drugs and losing all your worldly possessions while shattering the faith and confidence of your loved ones.

- Smoking cigarettes for over fifty years and ending up in the hospital with emphysema and lung cancer, with oxygen masks on your face and tubes running from your nose, but still sneaking out to smoke even though it is killing you.

- Pawning all of your valuables, charging up every credit card, borrowing money from friends and loved ones, only to waste it on the slots, roulette table, horses, or the bookie in the belief that this will make all your dreams and financial worries end.

•   Getting pregnant out of wedlock, and within a year, becoming pregnant again with no means by which to support yourself or the two children you have brought into the world.

There are many more examples, but I think you get my point. It's time to let go of the things of the world and let God take who we are and make us into what he wants us to be.

The Transformation of God

Once upon a time, there was a caterpillar named Sid. Now Sid was very ugly compared to all the animals in the forest, and all the other animals made fun of Sid. They talked about how many feet he had and about how ugly his 'fro" was, and they told him he looked like Buckwheat. Sid was always low. He would crawl in the dirt all day and hide from birds. He would always get sticks and twigs in his hairy body, which made his appearance even more unsightly. One day, Sid got this idea.

He thought, "I'll climb a tree and make myself a house." Sid climbed the tree and started to make a green house all over himself. All the animals really began making fun of Sid. They said that Sid must have really gone crazy now to get so high up and to build such an ugly house. Sid stayed in the house a long time and everyone thought he was dead. But one sunny day, the house began to move, and before anyone could say anything, a beautiful wing came out with so many colors that all the animals gasped with amazement. Then another wing came out. It was Sid, now a beautiful butterfly. He took off high into the sky and never crawled in the dirt again. He was transformed and renewed!

Oh how God loves even the little caterpillar, so how much more does he love us, His holy people? It is time for us to stop eating the devil's dirt and to let God's power transform us into super saints so that we can fly above the mediocrity of the devil and into the loving arms of Jesus! If you are *stuck on stupid*, or know someone who may be, God has a better plan for you and for them. The plan is found in His word, and it's time for you to find a church, to find a man or woman of God who can help you get the knowledge that will give you the power to be all that God wants you to be. Don't make the mistake of being so big in the world's eye and ending up being nothing in God's eye.

Orion Swett Marden said that the greatest thing a man can do in this world is to make the most possible out of the stuff that has been given to him. This is the definition of success, and there is no other. So if you have been given lemons, add the water and sugar from Jesus and make lemonade.

It is better to be part of a great whole than to be a whole of a small part, according to Frederick Douglass. When you let go and let God, you do just that, become part of the great whole.

Hurt People Tend to Hurt People

Grandmother Stevens (Della's grandmother) used to always tell me that a hurting person will always hurt you or hurt people, hurt people. When my baby girl, Kristina, was in the 6th grade, she was 5'11" tall. She's 6'2" now and an accomplished volleyball player. She wasn't very confident at the time, and she used to come home upset because her friends were talking about her, telling her that she was so skinny and so tall that she could hoola-hoop with a cheerio. She was so upset as a young 6th grader that I just felt compassion for her and wanted to give her some words of wisdom, words of encouragement that would keep her going. I told her to just keep drinking her milk, because milk does a body good, and one day she would grow up to be just like her mama.

I also told her that hurt people hurt other people in turn, that a person who is hurting will always try to pull you down to make themselves feel better about themselves. Anyone who doesn't feel good about themselves will always try to make you feel bad about yourself because they don't feel good about themselves. You have to learn sometimes to shake off some stuff. You have to tell them that they just need to learn to deal with it, that if they don't like you, it's not your problem but theirs and they just have to deal with it.

Grandmother Stevens used to always tell me that she marched with the dreamer, and the dreamer told her that one day we would live in a nation where a man is not judged by the color of his skin but by the content of his character. She used to always tell me that, if a person spits on you, it doesn't make you mad, it only makes you wet, and you have to choose to get mad about it. I can remember many times when, as a police officer, drunken people and others we would arrest would spit on us, and those words would always come back to me, ringing true in my mind. I would want to hit these people, but I would remember that I had a choice: to take that action or to let their ignorance go.

Grandmother Robinson a wonderful woman from the old neighborhood I grew up in Dallas would also tell us about this farmer who had a mule, and this mule used to follow the farmer around everywhere that he went. She used to say that the farmer loved that old mule so much that he would walk one half a mile a day down to the river to get that old mule some water. After the farmer got a little older and the mule got a little older, that walk down to the river got harder and harder. So the farmer decided to just dig himself a well right there in the middle of his farm. And sho' nuf, after a couple of days of digging, he wasn't able to finish that well because that old mule had fallen into the very hole that he was trying to complete for the mule.

When the farmer discovered that the old mule had fallen into the hole, he thought to himself: how in the world am I going to pull that old mule up. The farmer said, I can't shoot him. I can't bear to watch him die that way, and I can't pull him up because I'm not strong enough. So he decided, I'll just take the pile of dirt from the hole and throw it in on that old mule to put him out of his misery.

He turned his back to the hole and began to throw the dirt in on the old mule, shovel after shovel hitting the old mule on the head, and the old mule at the bottom of the hole began to go crazy. He started making all kinds of mule noises and thrashing at the bottom of the hole. As the farmer continued to throw dirt in the hole, the mule thought, if I continue to act like this, I'm going to die. Then a new thought came to his mind: every time that dirt hits me on my back, I'm going to shake it off and pack it under my feet. As that old farmer kept throwing dirt in on the mule, the mule began to rise, because the very thing that was meant to keep him down was the very thing that made him rise to success.

Now I don't know a lot about life, but I do know one thing: no weapon formed against us is going to destroy us unless we let it. I know that all things work for our good if we are called according to God's purpose — His purpose, not ours. He didn't say that all that happens to us would be good things, but rather that all things would work for the good. Because everything that is good *for* us, often times, is not good *to* us.

I have Attention Deficit Disorder (ADD). I also have a learning disability because my mom used drugs when I was in her womb. I also talk a lot, and the very thing that got me kicked out of class when I was young has become an asset to me. They used to kick me out of school, but now they pay me to go back into school and talk — God is good!

Many, many times people judge me based on the pigmentation of my skin, because I'm an African American, and I often speak to Caucasian and other non-African American students. Many times, I am prejudged before I go in, which results in this question: Can I relate to Caucasian students? They know that I am an ex-football player, which usually carries an additional stigma of not being able to communicate well and of not being intelligent. But I just shake all that stuff off, because I know that my purpose is to make a difference in children's lives. It is so interesting what happens when I get in the room and begin to share with some of those people who have prejudged me, as I articulate what God has given to me and speak of hope and wisdom to children. The very thing that they thought would keep me down has become the very thing that has elevated me up toward success. Just like the farmer's mule, I just keep stompin' the dirt and God brings me to the top.

You know that many are judging the people of our nation today who are of Arab decent, and of course 9-11 will rightfully go down in history as one of the worst tragedies ever in America. But the intolerant among us, the ignorant, are telling most of the Arab people to go back where they came from. It amazes me that Pearl Harbor, another tragedy, happened in the 1940s, and they did the same thing to Asian people. And in the 50s, 60s, and 70s, African Americans were targeted. The cycle simply does not seem to end.

For example, Hispanic people have been told for the last few decades to go back to Mexico, that they are taking all the jobs in America, which is the same great nation that lets different nationalities from all over the world come in. The statue of liberty, which after all represents a place, a nation, that embraces all cultures, says that if you bring us your tired and your hungry, those who have been downcast and forgotten, America will take them in. Consequently, it is astonishing to me that the same nation, the same people who themselves have ancestors who arrived here under similar circumstances, are now telling others to go back where they came from. But maybe I should not be surprised. Many of those same people's ancestors took the land from the Native Americans, after all. They came here on different ships, put people in slavery, and developed racist tendencies. But it is interesting that, when Timothy McVey bombed the Oklahoma City building, no one was telling white people to go back to Europe. You didn't see them telling Caucasian people, skinheads and racists, to go back to where they came from.

This is my response to all that brain-dead *stuck on stupid* separatist mentality that indeed separates us as people: We may have come here on separate ships, and some on deck and others in the hold in chains, but we are in the same boat now. We are all Americans, and together we stand and divided we fall. We are in this thing together, and this thing is called LIFE. We must understand that we have to come together and stop pulling each other down, stop allowing the devil to divide and conquer us, or we will never win this thing. The devil knows that he can't beat us if we ever really get together, that he can't destroy us if we are united. For all of God's people, all the people who are united in this great nation, under our great God, under the great banner of hope, must get together and stand tall.

CHAPTER TEN

I Told You So

"Don't be mislead; bad company corrupts good character. Come back to your senses as you ought, and stop sinning. For there are some who are ignorant of God, and I say this to your shame."

I Corinthians 15:33-34

In the six years that I served as a Tulsa Police Officer (1984-1990), I remember many people that I encountered who made a lasting impression on me. An encounter with one such person is a story that I tell children who are *stuck on stupid*, those who don't listen to wise counsel and hang around people with bad character. I tell them that they are going to get much more than they bargain for. It's a funny thing about sin: it will take you further than you want to go, keep you longer than you want to stay and make you pay much more than you want to pay.

One of my part-time jobs during this period in my life was serving as a security guard and part-time counselor in one of the inner-city high schools in Tulsa. I also ran the Fellowship of Christian Athletes (FCA) huddle, and I had many different kinds of students involved. This story is about one student in particular, a boy I found to be extremely gifted and talented who was the only young black man that I've ever met who I can honestly say could have been anything if he had put his mind to it.

For the sake of privacy, let's call him DW. DW had a photographic memory. He was a 4.0 student and on the honor roll every year since the first grade. He was a three sport letterman in football, basketball and wrestling, and he won the state championship in wrestling his junior and senior year. Not only was DW a great athlete, but all the girls wanted the chance to be exclusive with him. Many of the young men envied his good looks and outgoing personality. Simply stated, he was a pretty boy.

I knew that if I could get DW involved with the FCA group, he would not only be a tremendous addition to the group, but this young man could make a major impact for the Kingdom of God. However, DW had a darker side to his personality as I later discovered. He was a gang member with the RIP boys, a big time drug dealer and had absolutely no respect for authority, women or even life in general.

To put it in his own words: "I'm out just to get mine, and whoever I have to step on and whatever I have to do in the process makes me none (makes no difference to me)."

One day after an FCA meeting, DW arrived in a brand new red BMW to pick up one of the cheerleaders who regularly attended the meetings. Let's call her Candy. Candy was a very intelligent, talented and gifted athlete. She was not only a cheerleader but also ran track.

I asked DW where he got the new car, and his response was, "You know how it is, preach."

I responded, "I do. How much dope did you have to sell to get that? You can be anything you want to be, so why are you wasting your life and the life of others all in the name of money?"

DW pulled out a wad of one hundred dollar bills and stated, "This is my god. I know you are a preacher and everything, but this is what I trust in. It even says it on the bill: In God We Trust."

I looked at Candy and told her, "You better get away from DW. He is a snake and snakes bite."

Candy stated, "I love DW. He's my man. See all this gold? Anything I want, DW gets it for me."

I was later able to share with Candy the story about the Indian brave who went to the top of the tallest mountain in his land to prove his manhood. Once at the top of the mountain, it began to snow, and he covered himself with his big bearskin coat as the snow passed over. The next morning after rising, he found that a rattlesnake had crawled under the coat with him to keep warm.

Shocked, he jumped away from the snake and the snake said to him, "Don't be afraid. I won't bite. I need you. If I bite you, I won't have anybody to take me down from the snow. Can you take me down to the bottom of the mountain where it's nice and warm?"

The snake was very convincing with his smooth tongue. Full of pride and arrogance, the Indian brave thought, "I'm a man. I can conquer this mountain, and surely I can conquer this snake." So he picked up the snake and began his journey down the mountain. He and the snake had a wonderful conversation. He told the snake about how he would start his family once he got back to his tribe and how he would watch his children grow up as he grew old.

When they got to the bottom where it was nice and warm, he put the snake down on the nice warm ground. The snake graciously thanked him and began to slither away. The Indian brave then turned his back and the snake reversed his direction, coiled and bit the Indian brave on the leg.

The Indian screamed, "I thought you said you wouldn't bite me!!!!!!"

The snake responded as he slithered away, "You knew what I was when you picked me up. I'm a snake and snakes bite."

The Indian Brave fell over and died.

I said, "Candy, I told you DW was a snake, and when he bites you, I want you to remember that I told you so.

"You wrong, preacher, you wrong," she said. "DW loves me."

The next time I saw DW he let me know that Candy had shared what I had told her.

DW just laughed while holding a wad of money in his hand and stating, "I make more money in a month than you make in a year, preach. I'm gonna get paid and then get out of this game, and you're going to be working the rest of your life on a dead end job for the white man, who don't give a f---! about you."

DW's gang had about fifty members, and some of our narcotics agents had discovered that any given month DW and his gang were making $50,000 to $100,000 per month selling crack cocaine. I knew that trying to reason with him was out of the question. I asked him to meet me the next day because I had a going away present for him. It was DW's senior year, and he had received a full scholarship in wrestling at one of the top Oklahoma colleges, but he could have gone on an academic or athletic scholarship. The next day, I purchased a red pillow and had the words "I Told You So" embroidered on it. When DW came to pick Candy up from school, I met him with the pillow and gave it to him.

He asked, "What is this?"

"If you don't change your way of living, you're going to end up lying on a pillow like this in a casket or biting one as some big 300 pound inmate makes you bite it so no one can hear you scream while he's raping you. They like pretty boys like you in prison," I said.

DW cussed me out, threw the pillow at me and stated, "It will never happen to me, bet that."

DW did go to college, but after a year he was kicked out for a confrontation he had with a rival gang member who was a football player at the same university. DW came back to Tulsa, took his gang from fifty members to over 200, and went from $50,000 to $100,000 per month to over $500,000 per month. He bought houses, cars, jewelry, and gave big parties. DW was the king drug dealer in Tulsa. Candy became one of his main drug runners and distributors but also his best user. Little did he know that undercover DEA agents and local law enforcement had infiltrated his gang, and after a year-long investigation, DW's kingdom came tumbling down. He was arrested, and all of his cars, houses, jewelry and money were seized. Many of his boys testified against him. The undercover agents had over 75 separate cases of major drug distribution on him, linking him all the way to Columbia.

Four months after his arrest, he was being sentenced, and guess who was sitting in the courtroom with the pillow. The

judge sentenced him to life plus sixty years in a federal peniten-
tiary, which means that if DW dies and comes back to life he
has to go back to prison for sixty more years. As they escorted
him out of the courtroom, I raised the pillow, pointed to it and
smiled. I had no compassion for him. I had tried to tell him, but
now he would find out for himself that you reap what you sow.

I wish I could say that this was the last time I saw DW.
In 1991, after being on staff with FCA in Indiana for one year, I
was asked to go to Oklahoma and play a basketball game with an
FCA team against the inmates and afterwards to share my testimony. While playing in the game, there were some men dressed
like women sitting on the front bottom row in the gym. One of
them screamed, "Hey preacher," as I ran by.

I didn't want to look, but as I glanced from the corner of
my eye there was something familiar about the person. He made
several attempts to get my attention, but I ignored him. After the
game, as they were setting up for the service, they also invited
anyone who wanted to stay to come down. The young man who
had been trying to get my attention walked toward me. He had
his hair pulled back and tied in a bun on top of his head. He also
wore eye makeup and lipstick, and his shorts were so short that
they exposed the bottom of his buttocks. He wore a t-shirt tied
up in a ball in the middle of his stomach, and he had flip-flops
on, which showed his painted toe nails. As he got closer, I recognized him as DW!

He asked if I remembered him. I said that I did and asked
him if he would be staying for the service. He said that his man
wouldn't let him. I didn't feel like I felt in the courtroom. All
I could think was what a waste. I felt sick to my stomach and
asked if I could pray for him. He said yes, and for the first time I
can honestly say that I didn't know what to pray. So I asked one
of the staff members to pray for him.

After the prayer, DW looked at me and stated, "You told
me so, but I didn't listen." A 6'7", 350 pound muscle-bound,

bald headed, BIG black man screamed for DW to come here, and when DW walked over to him, he picked him up by his pants, tongue kissed him, put him down and patted him on his buttocks.

He then pointed to me, stating, "If you come in here, you gonna be my woman too."

To that I responded, "That's why I'm leaving. You don't ever have to worry about me coming back unless it's to preach the word."

If DW's story ended here, it would be tragic enough, but the story gets even worse. People generally ask, "What happened to Candy?" A couple of days after ministering in the prison, I decided to ride with one of my former police partners back in Tulsa to catch up on old times. At the time, we were patrolling an area known for prostitution and drug traffic. We received a call to investigate a young lady who appeared to be highly intoxicated walking in the middle of the street with a baby in her arms. We arrived on the scene and exited the police car to find a young lady who was under the influence of some type of drug, maybe crack or heroin, and alcohol. She had a pair of white pants on that were so dirty they appeared to be brown, with a bikini swimsuit top and dirty white tennis shoes with no socks. Her hair was uncombed, and she looked and smelled like she hadn't taken a bath in at least one month. The baby she carried in her arms was about seven months old, with only a dirty diaper. The young lady was approximately 5'9" and weighed 90 pounds. She was very, very thin, a clear sign that she was undernourished and maybe addicted to drugs. The young lady looked very familiar, but I couldn't remember how I knew her.

She was so high that she didn't recognize that I was with a uniformed police officer, and she walked up to me and stated that she would perform a sexual act for me for money. She then asked if I wanted to buy her baby. She was immediately arrested and her baby transported to child services. On our way to the jail to book her, she began to cry uncontrollably, asking us to give her a second chance. The officer I was with began to ascertain her personal information for the police report, and after giving her real name, it hit me: it was Candy!! I asked if she remembered attending this high school and if she used to date DW.

She looked at me and said, "Preacher!"

She seemed to come out of the daze she was in, and I asked what happened to her.

"After DW was arrested I was hooked on crack because I could get all I wanted for free." I responded, "But it really wasn't free, was it?"

She then said she began dating some of DW's gang members and got pregnant, and in two years she had two babies. She was on welfare and began selling herself to meet the need of her drug habit.

Then she said those words I will never forget: "You told me DW was a snake, and I didn't listen."

At this time in my life, I had a daughter who was almost five years old, and all I could think of was: what if this was my baby girl? I remember how beautiful Candy used to be and how this association with one person could so devastate her life and her future. I asked if there was anything I could do for her, and she said she was too far gone for any help. We arrived at the police station, booked her, and I gave her my card and some numbers for local ministries that would be willing to assist her and her baby. I can remember crying as I walked back to the car, thinking to myself that the devil is a liar and deceiver.

After returning to Indianapolis, I didn't think much about Candy until I would tell a story about her and DW. In 1993, the former partner I was riding with the night I saw Candy informed me that she had been found dead of an overdose in an abandoned apartment that known drug users used to shoot up and get high.

I tell young people all the time that they are our future today because what they do today will ultimately determine their tomorrow. If you want to know what your tomorrow is going to look like, just look around and see who you're following today.

Keep Fighting

I tell children all the time that no one is born a winner or a loser; we are born choosers. Every choice that you make can have a positive or negative effect on your destiny. So, as a result, you must watch your thoughts, because your thoughts become your words. You must watch your words because they become your actions. You must watch your actions because they become your habits. And you must watch your habits because they become your character. And you must watch your character because it becomes your destiny. Your faith plus your values plus your decision making process equals your character. Proverbs 13:18-20 says, "He who ignores discipline comes to poverty and shame. Whoever heeds correction is honored. And a longing fulfilled is sweet to the soul, but fools detest training from evil. Any man who walks with the wise grows wise, but a companion of fools suffers harm."

You know, we read in the paper and we hear on the air of stealing and killing and crime everywhere. We sigh and we say, as we notice this trend, that this young generation's where it all will end. Too much money to spend, too much idle time, too many movies of passion and crime, too many books not fit to be read, and too much evil in what we have said. Too many children encouraged to do wrong, and too many parents who won't stay at home. Kids don't make the movies, and they don't write the books. They don't paint the pictures of gangsters and crooks; they don't make the liquor and they don't run the bars; they don't make the laws and make high-speed cars; and they don't make the drugs that rattle the brain. It's all done by old folks greedy for gain. Thus in so many cases it must be confessed that the labeled delinquent is the old folks' best.

Children become who they are programmed to be. And as I travel around the country, I often remind the leaders, the people who have been called to program the children into what they need to become. First and foremost, you must be different, because you turn into what programs you. So many children don't understand that their destiny starts with whom they associate. We have to warn them by helping them identify things that will pull them up and we can't let the devil and the things of this world to continue to pull them down. We must keep fighting.

Children learn what they live. If a child lives with criticism, he learns to condemn. If a child lives with hostility, he learns to fight. If a child lives with jealousy, he learns to hate. If a child lives with ridicule, he learns to be sharp. If a child lives with fear, he learns to be apprehensive. If a child lives with shame, he learns to feel guilty. If a child lives with tolerance, he learns to be patient. If a child lives with encouragement, he learns to be confident. If a child lives with praise, he learns to appreciate. If a child lives with approval, he learns to like himself. And if a child lives with acceptance and friendship, he learns that the world is a nice place in which to live and love.

One of my favorite Chinese proverbs is: one who thinks he is leading and has no one following is only taking a walk. That is so true. If leadership is simply the ability to obtain followers, then why are so many of our children being led astray? Leaders aren't stepping up and doing what they are supposed to do. Hitler was a leader, and so was Jim Jones, but so were Jesus of Nazareth, Martin Luther King, Jr., Winston Churchill and John F. Kennedy. And while their value systems were all different, each of these positive leaders had followers. And I'm telling you right now, I told you so. Until we stand up and show our children which way to go, they won't know which way to go. God is calling on us, the leaders of our community, to stand up and lead the way by first identifying that we need the way inside of us. And when we do this, our children will learn to love and not hate, to come together and heal and not hurt. We have to keep on keeping on.

Proverbs 12:1, "Whoever loves discipline loves knowledge, but whoever hates correction is stupid."

Are You Stuck On Stupid?

In the Power to Conform chapter I discussed where the phrase *stuck on stupid* came from. For the rest of my life, I think that statement will be a part of me. Everywhere I go, teachers say that they remember that statement, not to be *stuck on stupid*. So I developed a little list so that maybe we can identify children who may be *stuck on stupid* and help them get unstuck by giving them knowledge. Eight ways to tell if you may be *stuck on stupid*:

1. The *stuck on stupid* person reacts and blames all their problems on their parents or teachers — it's everyone else's fault. They are the victims and they take no responsibility for their life. They never stop to think. This person never has a plan; they just react to negative or positive criticism.

2. The *stuck on stupid* person begins with no end in mind. Like I said, they never have a plan. They avoid all goals at all cost and never think about tomorrow. They live for the moment, sleep around and get wasted, partying non-stop for tomorrow they might die. I saw some of these children in one of the upper-middleclass schools in California. After I finished talking, some of the children came up to me and basically asked, "Why plan for tomorrow when you don't think you are going to live through

today?" So just party till you die was their philosophy, which is the mentality out there today.

3. The *stuck on stupid* person does not coop-
erate. These people think that just because
people feel distant or different than they do
that they are weird or out of touch, so why get
along with them. These people feel that they
always have the best ideas, and thus doing
things their way is the only way. Yes, they are
out there, most from the ME generation, those
people that believe that it makes no sense to follow anyone because they could die tomorrow.

4. The *stuck on stupid* person puts first things
last. This person always feels that they are the
most important things in life and don't do what
needs to be done until they have wasted time
watching TV, videos, talking on the phone, and
surfing the net. They always put off their own
work until tomorrow and recognize no structure or discipline. My question is: where do
they learn that? The answer is from older people who put no structure or parameters on them.

5. The *stuck on stupid* person thinks win/lose.
They see life as a vicious competition that
they must win and everyone else must lose,
and they look at life as if they are going to
lose and make sure that they are going to drag
as many people down with them as possible.

6. The *stuck on stupid* person always wants
to take the easy way out. They are just lazy:

at home, at school, at work. They look for the shortcuts. They could care less about their grades, or what people think and feel about them. They just take life easy and have no goals.

7. The *stuck on stupid* person is the first to talk and then pretend to listen. They feel that they were born with a mouth so they must use it. They always talk, always express their side of the story first, and then pretend to listen by nodding their head and saying, uh huh, uh huh. But you know instantly that this person could care less about what you had to say. They simply got their point out and that is all that matters to them.

8. The *stuck on stupid* people wear themselves out. They stay so busy with life that they never take time off to renew themselves. They never study. They never ask for help. They don't exercise, and they don't eat properly. They are constantly going like the little rat on the wheel of life, going real fast but not going anywhere. It kind of reminds me of the Indy 500 race: going 500 miles to end up the same place that you started and then celebrating a goal that was no real destination. The trouble with the rat race of life is that even if you win you're still a rat.

We must help our children by helping them discover the potential that is inside them. We must help them to use their creative imagination, and show them that they can have a goal. We must help them to magnify their integrity in order to trust and believe in everybody else. We must help them by making them take responsibility for their actions. We must let them know that you must clarify your identify before you can change your actions. So as a man thinketh, so is he. You must help them to understand that eagles are not like chickens. Eagles spread their wings and use adversity for opportunity. Remember that the same winds that will blow other birds down, the eagles simply adjust their wings to and use to fly higher. We must help our children by helping them stay focused, by giving them goals, by helping them dream big dreams.   To soar like an eagle we must help them by thinking positively, because if you think you can or you think you can't, you are right in either case. We must help them know that they are better than what this world tells them that they are. They are not chicken heads and they are not hood rich. They are not thugs, no matter what this world tells them that they are going to be. A popular song entitled "I'm a Thug" by the artist Trick Daddy, states in one part of the song "I don't know what this world's gonna be but I know one thing that this is the life for me, baby cause I'm a thug. All day, every day, baby cause I'm a thug. Wouldn't change for the world baby cause I'm a thug." We must tell and convince our youth that the thug life is not the life for them they are more that just a thug. They are more than conquerors for Him who loves them and has called them for a mighty purpose.

CHAPTER ELEVEN

Look Up to Get the Hookup

You Need a Dream Team

"I lift up mine eyes to the hills, for where does my help come from? My help comes from the Lord. The maker of the Heavens and the Earth."

Ps. 121:1

"The Lord said to him, get up, take up your bed and walk."

John 5:8

Attitude is everything, because your attitude determines your altitude if you have persistence, courage, and fortitude. And we all need somebody to lean on. Grandmother Stevens used to always tell me that every day is unique. No day will ever curve from its course or be repeated. At midnight, all days are going to end, quietly, certainly, totally, and forever. But the hours between now and then are opportunities with eternal possibility. She used to say that you will never again worship your Lord or share His love with someone today. But with His enablement, we can live each day to the fullest as if it were our last day on earth. Because it may well be.

Between the ages of one and eighty, we have 29,200 days to live. For the sake of comparison, let's say that at the age of one God gave every individual $29,200 on which to live for the next 79 years, and he told them that was it. Everything they had to wear, drive, eat, or live in came out of that $29,200. You couldn't invest it, and no one could give us anything else. The question then becomes: how would we treat that money, knowing today that this is all we will be allowed for our lives, as mature adults? Like so many people, we take advantage, or we don't take advantage as the case may be, of the opportunities that we have. And then as a result we get way down the line and discover that we are almost out of time. That's why we have to take advantage of every opportunity that we have to pull one another up and encourage each other to look to the hills from whence cometh our help, and our help does come from the Lord. God uses His people to help His people.

An anonymous prayer that I picked up at an FCA camp years ago that I have added to my life most every morning is "Keep me faithful, keep me grateful, and this is my earnest plea each day. Keep me serving, keep me teaching of his love while yet I may. Serving Christ under law may be a duty, but serving him under love is a delight."

I try to live my life as a thermostat versus being a thermometer. A thermometer changes to the temperature of its environment and a thermostat sets the temperature for the environment. I have found that my attitude helps me set a positive environment in any and every situation I find myself in. This means that, when I show up in a situation, the situation adjusts to my attitude and I do not allow the circumstances to adjust my attitude. I try to always be a difference maker, and making a difference starts with the way we perceive ourselves — because truly attitude is everything.

Charles Swindol states in a handout I received at church,

> "The longer I live, the more I realize the impact of attitude on life. It is more important than the past, than the facts of any given situation, than education and money, than current circumstances, than failures and successes or what people think, say or do. Attitude is more important than a parent's gift or skill, and it will make or break a company, church or a home. The remarkable thing is that we have a choice every day, regardless of the attitude that we embrace for that day. We cannot change our past or the fact that a person is acting a certain way; we cannot change the inevitable. The only thing we can play is the one string that we have, and that is our attitude. And I am convinced that life is 10% what happens to me and 90% how I respond to it. And so it is with you. We are all in charge of our attitudes."

Ephesians 4:23 tells us "to be made new in the attitude of our minds." I believe that our attitude is our most important asset. John Maxwell states in his book *The 21 Irrefutable Laws of Leadership* "A leader's attitude is caught by his or her followers more

quickly than his or her actions, and it is just as contagious."¹ We
see what we are prepared to see, so what are we prepared to see
in the people who are following us? What are we prepared to do
to allow God to work through and in us? Expectations make the
difference, and our expectations have a great deal to do with our
attitudes.

Leadership has less to do with position than it does with
disposition. A recent survey conducted by the Center of Leadership Development in 2002 indicates that people with emotional
problems are 144% more likely to have automobile accidents
than those who are emotionally stable. Another alarming fact re-
vealed by this study is that one out of every five victims of fatal
accidents had a quarrel within six hours of his or her accident.
This leads me to believe that our attitudes are caught as well as
taught. Too often, as a man thinks, so is he.

We must begin to think that we are born to be winners
not losers because we can't lose with the stuff we use when we
choose the right stuff and part of the right stuff is choosing to
have a positive attitude. Maxwell states again "It is amazing that
the pessimist complains about the wind and the optimist expects
it to change, but the leader simply adjusts the sail, and the sail
that needs adjusted is what is in his mind."² We cannot choose
how many years we may live, but we can choose how much life
those years will contain. We cannot control the beauty of our
face, but we can control the expression that is on it. We cannot
control life's most difficult moment, but we can choose to make
life less difficult. We cannot control the negative atmosphere of
the world, but we can control the atmosphere of our minds. Too
often, we try to control things that we can't, and too seldom we
choose to control what we can: our attitude. It is not what happens to me that matters, but what happens in me. God chooses
what we go through, but we choose how we go through it. It is
not "why" that we should always ask, but "what." The leader's
attitude helps determine the attitude of the follower, so are you

a thermostat or a thermometer? Your attitude will often times determine the answer to that question. When opportunity knocks at the door, a positive person opens the door with his arms wide open, rejoicing that opportunity has come. But when opportunity knocks at the door for a negative person, he complains about the noise. "Attitude simply determines altitude — if we have persistence, courage and fortitude." Coach Lucious Newhouse, my high school track coach. This was the first time I heard that.

From the Success Series

Attitude is everything. Attitude is the way we think. Attitude is something other people can actually see. They can hear it in your voice, see it in the way that you move, feel it when they are with you. Your attitude expresses itself in everything you do all the time, wherever you are. A positive attitude invites positive results, and a negative attitude always invites negative results. Attitude makes a difference every hour, everyday, and in everything you do. For your entire life, what you get out of each thing you do will equal the attitude you have when you do it. Anything you do with a positive attitude will work for you. Anything you do with a negative attitude will work against you. If you have a positive attitude, you are looking for ways to solve problems you can solve and you are letting go of things over which you have no control. You can develop a positive attitude by simply emphasizing the good, by being tough-minded, and by refusing defeat.

The persistence that we need comes from God, and we can run with perseverance. Someone who gets up even when they can't, perseveres and has the never, never, never quit mentality. This person has the courage to stay the course, and sometimes you have to make waves of your own. Courage is never being afraid, but standing in the face of fear. It is fortitude, firmness in facing failure, pain, danger or trouble. It is firmness of the spirit, and our God has not given us the spirit of fear but of love and of courage and a sound mind.

Persistence

Nothing in the world can take the place of persistence. Talent will not. Nothing is more common than unsuccessful men with talent. DW was an excellent example of this fact. Genius will not either, and unrewarded genius is almost a proverb. Education will not trump persistence; the world is full of educated derelicts. Persistence and determination alone are omnipotent. Persistence prevails when all else fails. We can fly because we think we can fly. And the more the winds blow, the more we simply adjust our wings — which is simply our attitude — and use adversity for opportunity.

The Winner vs. Loser

The winner is always a part of the answer; the loser is always a part of the problem. The winner always has a program; the loser always has an excuse. The winner says, "Let me do it for you." The loser says, "That's not my job." The winner sees an answer for every problem; the loser sees a problem for every answer. The winner sees a green at every sand trap; the loser sees two or three sand traps near every green. The winner says, "It may be difficult, but it is possible." The losers says, "It may be possible, but it is too difficult." Be a winner, not a whiner. Get rid of that "stinkin' thinkin'." Think big. Think success. Think positive.

The difference between successful people and others is not a lack of strength, not a lack of knowledge, but rather a lack of will. When was the last time you willed yourself to win refusing defeat, refusing to quit no matter the cost? You may have been knocked down but you weren't out. Down on the mat dazed but not out. If circumstances and your situation looks unsurmountable at this moment but I want to tell you, if you're down and not out you're still in the fight, look for your corner for the people encouraging you to get up. Shake off the dizziness, the embarrassment of being knocked down and make your way to the corner take your standing eight and listen to the instruction of the people who really have your back. And above all get back in the fight and keep swinging to win.

Don't Quit

When things go wrong, as they sometimes will,
When the road you're trudging seems all uphill,
When the funds are low and the debts are high,
And you want to smile, but you have to sigh,
When cares are pressing you down a bit,
Rest if you must, but do not quit.

Life is queer with its twists and turns,
As every one of us sometimes learns,
And many persons are turned about,
When they might have won had they stuck it out.
Don't give up though the pace seems slow,
You may succeed with another blow.

Often the struggler has given up,
When he may have captured the victor's cup,
And he learned too late when the night came down,
How close he was to the golden crown.
Success is failure turned inside out,
So stick with the fight when you're hardest hit.
It's when things seem worse that you mustn't quit.

Anonymous

Prime Rib: Prime People

When I think of people that have had an impact on me in my life none other has had a greater impact than the woman I married February 19, 1983, my wife Della, my "Prime Rib". I call her that because when God made Eve He did so from one of Adam's ribs. Back in college, she raised my level of expectation by giving me dreams, big dreams. She would never accept mediocrity inside of me. She has been my best friend and more than a friend: my lover, my confidant, my encourager. Sometimes, she has also been my mother, my provider, my guider, and my hope. She has been one of, if not the most significant person in my life outside of the person of Christ.

I think back on my life, and I think about the tests that we've all encountered. I think about how different people responded. Answer these questions: name the five wealthiest people in the world; name at least five Heisman trophy winners; name at least five winners of the Miss America contest pageant; name ten people who have won the Noble Prize; name at least one-half dozen Academy Award winners for best actor or actress; name the last decade's World Series winners. What these questions indicate is that none of us remember the headliners of yesterday. These are not second place achievers. They are the best in their field. But the applause dies, awards tarnish, achievements are forgotten. Accolades and certificates are buried with their owners. However, many of us can list the teachers who aided us in our journey. We can name friends that have helped us through difficult times. We can name people that have taught us something worthwhile. We can think of few people who have made us feel appreciated. We can think of people with whom we have enjoyed spending time. We can name dozens of heroes whose stories have inspired us.

The people who make a difference in our lives are not

the ones who are most celebrated for their money or their fame. They are the ones who care for us. My wife has been that inspiration of hope. No greater union has been created in my life than the union that was formed when I took Ms. Della Sanders to be my wife, for better or worse, for richer or poorer, in sickness and in health and until death do we part.

It has not always been easy but our love for each other and our love for Christ has and will continually see us through. We set out on a journey together to raise children in the fear and admonition of the Lord, to stand together in the midst of tough times and we're sure there will be more to come. We keep looking up, and God gives us the attitude that we are more than a conqueror, that we can do all things through Christ who strengthens us. Greater is He that is in us, than he that is in the world. Together we stand and divided we fall we're in this thing together; this thing is called life. Life is not only for ourselves, but for our children, our community and for our world. Those who follow after are a team that we are called to minister to. For the vision, I thank God. I thank him that he has allowed me such a dreamer, allowed me such a person in my life. She is my number one dream builder. She soars with me.

Dream = Team

To achieve your dream you need a team

If your mind can conceive it, and you firmly believe, with the right team you can achieve it. Nothing just happens; God uses people to bless people. I tell children all the time that in the midst of their dream they must be:

D	=	**Daring and Disciplined**
R	=	**Respectful and Responsible**
E	=	**Excellent in Education**
A	=	**Attitude to Achieve**
M	=	**Motivation to Move**

Daring and Disciplined

To be daring and disciplined in relationship to being on a team means that everyone needs to follow those who are placed ahead of us. But we need some people who are willing to stand up and go against the grain. I can remember coming out of the academy, a young man full of God and full of hope, determined to make a difference as a police officer. I also remember getting into many heated discussions with many of the facilitators in the academy, about religion and about God and relationships. They would try to degrade those men who made mistakes from a spiritual perspective in order to justify the things that police officers do. I took an oath before God and country, and I simply asked this question: "What does it mean to take an oath before a God if we didn't completely clarify who He is?"

I remember the men in our squad room; the profanity and smoking. I took a stand that I was going to stay united with my wife, but 90% of the men in my squad had been through a divorce or were alcoholics. The stress of the job had gotten to them. I was daring enough to stand up and proclaim the gospel in the midst of men who were called to create peace but who had no peace in their own lives. I was daring enough to go against the grain and not indulge in all the sinful activity that many of the police officers around me were indulging in. Daring enough to stand up for Christ. Many times, I was ridiculed and talked about, but eventually some of those same men needed answers to problems that they were going through and came back to me for advice, the very man they were criticizing.

God will make your enemy your footstool. I was disciplined enough to keep my body and my mind and soul together. These lessons were an extension of what I had learned from football, training and conditioning myself, pushing through pain and adversity, because no discipline at the time seems pleasant but is profitable and useful in the end.

Respectful and Responsible

To respect myself and respect others was sometimes hard, because I didn't have respect for women growing up. However, now I am teaching my daughter that young men will treat you the way you let them. I am teaching my sons that you stand up in the midst of turmoil and respect yourself and respect women. I tell them that you treat others the way that you would want someone to treat your daughter or the way you would want someone to treat your mother. There is a mentality out there today from the pimps and some media that tells the young men that a true player needs a wife, a mistress and a whore. And I ask those pimps a question: "Which one of those would you want your mama to be?"

Excellence in Education

My ninth grade English teacher, Mrs. Woods had us memorize "Good, better and best, never let it rest, until your good becomes better and your better becomes best". Our attitude does determine our altitude, if we have courage, persistence and fortitude. And if you have a dream, that must keep you moving, that's what motivates you. If your dream is not big enough to keep you moving, you need to keep dreaming bigger.

I am reminded of Coach Newhouse, my track coach in the midst of running hills asked me the question, "was it worth it?" I didn't understand what he was asking me at the time because there was pain going through my body, my knees, back and toes were hurting and I thought that everything in me was breaking down. He kept asking, "was it worth it?" He made me stop and asked me this question, "Why are you out here running? Why are you out here punishing yourself like this?"

I said, "Because I want to win state and be the best. I want to be the first in my family to attend college and do something with my life."

And he looked at me and said, "Is it worth it? Is it worth all the running, all the lifting, all the studying, and all the things that you need to go through?

And if it's not you need to dream bigger that's why I have you running these hills because in life you have to learn how to conquer your hills."

I never will forget that. Your dreams are like hills the bigger they are the harder the climb but once you get to the top it's worth all the effort it took to get there. Sometimes in the midst of your climbing you will slip and begin to fall and it seems all you can do is reach and grab and hold on to a ledge. God has never called us to hold on, but to be more than conquerors. However, if you are holding on, just don't let go. Hold on to your dream. That dream will encourage you to higher. Hold on to the dreams that give you the strength to pull yourself up when things go bad.

Dr. Martin Luther King, Jr. was a dreamer. He encouraged others to climb the mountains of despair. He said in his I have a dream speech that one day this nation will rise up and live out the true meaning of it's creed.

> "We hold these truths to be self-evident, that all men are created equal. I have a dream that one day on the red hills of Georgia, the sons of former slaves and the sons of former slave-owners will be able to sit down together at the table of

brotherhood."

When you read the entire speech he refers to the mountains of Tennessee, the molehills of Mississippi and he talks about freedom ringing from every mountainside. He ends with,

"When we let freedom ring, when we let it ring from every village and every hamlet, from every state and every city, we will be able to speed up that day when all of God's children, black men and white men, Jews and Gentiles, Protestants and Catholics, will be able to join hands and to sing in the words of the old Negro spiritual, Free at last, free at last, thank God Almighty we're free at last."

Freedom isn't free it always comes with a price but it's always worth what you have to pay to get what you desire.

Motivation to Move

Your dreams are what keep you motivated. But I too have a dream, a dream that all of God's people will realize the power that they possess and that by dreaming in Him, letting Him work through us, will accomplish all that He can do in and through us. That is when we will truly come together.

I have a dream that kids will stop killing one another. I have a dream that young teenage girls who buy the lie from young men will wake up and realize that love is not lying down out of wedlock, but getting a ring on your finger, and papers, and a name. I have a dream that young men who are killing other young men in the streets will wake up and understand that all life is valuable. I have a dream that in every school that I enter teachers will become encouraged to pull children up and not allow despair of this world to pull them down. I have a dream that daddies will come home and that mothers will fall in love with daddies again and that children will walk after the example that daddies set.

Who Was Dad?

Was he a man that was never there?
A man that had no time to share.
A man that could always provide,
But never took our hands to guide.
A man that gave love to others
But never any to my sister or brother.
When life is over and journey's through
Which one will they say of you?
Tell me who was Dad?

Was he a man that was always there?
A man who always showed he cared?
A man who always had a word from God,
But never spared his loving rod?
A man who loved his childern and wife
And always led them by the fruit of his life?
When life is over and journey's through
Which one will they say of you?
Who was Dad?

I hope and pray that my children say
That dad loved Jesus till his dieing day.
And if we trust him He would lead the way.
So life is too short just for living and dieing
Tell me who is the father of your heart?
One day life will be over for you
Which one will they say was true?
Tell me who was Dad?

Ken Johnson

Yes, I have a dream that my children will grow up respectable, God-fearing people. The example that we set for them will be enough for them to start a new hope for their children, and their children's children. And if God should tarry before he comes to take us home, my children can be a part of changing the level of expectation in our nation.

Oh, I have a dream, a dream that the life that we live today will truly make a difference for tomorrow, that we will be sure of what we hope for but search what we don't see. Are you a dream builder, or are you a dream killer? Simply determined are your fruits. He is the vine, we are the branches, and He calls some of us to be gardeners, vine-dressers, cutting away the things that so easily entangle us and running with the perseverance and for the hope of Christ.

To have a dream is one thing, but to take action is something entirely different. To see far is one thing, but to go far is another thing entirely. There are three types of people: people who make things happen, people who watch things happen, and people who wonder what happened. The greatest athletes say that the hardest part of practicing is getting in the gym or on the field. To begin is to be half done. Actually, what separates us? Dream builders are people of action, those who go forth not allowing the circumstances and situations to pull us down. That is all that separates us.

I want you to stop right now, make a list, and think back on all the people who have had an impact on your life, those who helped pull you up. The dream builders who have changed you for the better. Write their names down. If you know where they are, I want you to contact them and tell them what they did to make a difference in your life. I want you to tell them how they have pulled you up. They need to be encouraged and thanked for the contribution that they have made in your life. Try your best to contact those people at all costs. If they were teachers, try to look up the old schools where they taught. If they were parents or pastors or just friends who have had an impact on you, it is important that you tell them. Make every effort that you can to contact those dream builders and encourage them to keep doing what they are doing to make a difference. By letting them know that they touched one, and that person is you, then truly, truly they will be encouraged to keep going on.

To my lovely wife who has been not only my inspiration, motivation and encouragement to keep on keeping on in the midst of all the mountains called us to climb. Your love and faith gives me the strength to climb, to fight and never quit no matter the odds or circumstances that may be against us. Just know I can't lose with the stuff I use and God has given you to me to be a part of right stuff I need to keep me going for him.

CHAPTER TWELVE

Keep on Pulling

"For even if I boast, somewhat freely about the authority the Lord gave us for building you up, rather than pulling you down, I will not be ashamed of it."

2 Corinthians 10:8

As you will recall from the story of the eagle, one day the little eagle was pulled from the coop by another eagle and placed upon a hill. We all need someone in our lives who will help pull us up, and dream builders pull us up while dream killers try to pull us down. I have many people in my life who have helped pull me up. One such dream builder was my coach in high school, Coach Newhouse, who told me that hard work would be the key to getting out of the inner city and out of that impoverished mentality I had descended into unwittingly. I was somewhat lazy when it came to many things, because I had been conditioned to take the easy way out. Being surrounded by mediocrity will condition you that way, and it can affect anyone at any point in life. Consequently, we all need people in our life who will not give up on us. Just like the little eagle that was in the coop, another eagle came by and pulled me up out of the same kind of condition, out of the cage that trapped me.

Coach Newhouse used to tell me, "Mr. Johnson, I want you to be the first one on the field and the last one to leave, and I want you to do one more of everything than everybody else." He told me that the result of my hard work would be that I would not have to worry about success, because success would take care of itself. So I can remember rushing from class, hurrying to put my clothes on to be the first on the field. I respected Coach Newhouse because he was a man who always kept his word and always showed a real concern for me. He was one of the first men to really convince me that I could be more than some thug from the ghetto. I remember the many, many, many days that I kept a log of everything that everyone else did, which I would then go through after practice to make sure I did one more of every drill. I made it a point to be the last one off the field, and this coach's advice and my effort were why I became a Blue Chip All-American football player and broke many records in track and field. God has truly elevated me because hard work kills laziness. I tell young people all the time, "If you want to kill laziness, you need two words: hard work." Hard work is simply pushing past taking the easy way out, going the extra mile. When others want to give up, you keep on going.

There is a song that came out in the summer of 2002 entitled "Hood Rich" by Big Timers. The hook was,

> "Gator boots with the pimped out Gucci suit. Ain't got no job, but I stay sharp. Can't pay my rent all my moneys spent. But that's okay, but I stay fly. Got a quarter tank of gas, in my new e-class, but that's all right cause I'm gonna ride. Got everything in my mamma's name, but I'm hood rich, na na na na na na na."

This song really depicts the mentality of many people today: rappers boasting about not having jobs but being sharp, boasting about not being able to pay their rent but how that's ok because they're still fly; boasting about their brand new Mercedes Benz. However the word of God tells us that if a man doesn't work he shouldn't eat. There is a direct correlation between working and eating. So if you want to eat, you must work. The mentality today is to have instant riches, however, what I call the lottery mentality.

Well, my response to those with the "hood rich" mentality is: "Selling dope may give you all your hope. Think you cool because you can cruise, think you fly because you get high but don't be surprised when your friends die. I told you so. You're *stuck on stupid* for sho! 'Cause you don't know you reap what you sow. So turn it around and stop pulling people down. You better get you a dream and get on the right team."

The Ms. Woods story

Ms Woods is one of those unique teachers that come into

a young man's life perhaps once in a lifetime. She was 5 ft. nothing and 100 pounds of nothing, but she was a fireball. A classic example of the adage that dynamite truly does come in small packages. She was my ninth grade English teacher. Now Ms. Woods was one of those ladies who would not allow you to accept mediocrity.

I tell the kids when I speak to them about the time Ms. Woods saw me running in the hall one day. She knew that I played on the football varsity, but she was astonished to see me going into the LD English class because of my ADD I mentioned earlier. Ms. Woods thought it appalling that someone with my potential and ability would be in a learning disability class. But after researching the topic and learning from Coach Newhouse that I had the potential to go to college, Ms. Woods made it her personal mission, from her perspective, to pull me up.

I can remember it like yesterday: She came into the LD class and told the teacher that I would be transferred from LD to her class. I felt excitement as well as fear at this news. I was excited because I was leaving the LD class and the stigma associated with individuals who were in the class. The lesson plan was easy, and there was no level of expectation for the lesson set before you. But I was afraid because I was going into the regular English class, and at the time I was not a good reader or speller. I was intimidated. She took me from my chicken coop and put me on the mountain by raising the level of expectation she had for me.

I am often reminded of many of the things that my grandmother and many other people have told me. One of the most important is that when you need courage is when you are afraid. Sometimes in life, you will be afraid, but be of good cheer, be of good courage, because our Lord has not given us the spirit of fear but of love, power and a sound mind. When you are *stuck on stupid*, however, you don't understand that even though trapped in your coop there are people who will come to pull you up.

They don't come to hurt you, but to pull you past mediocrity. Ms. Woods was trying to do this for me, but I didn't understand. Part of me wanted to cluck and stay in the LD class, but another part of me wanted to fly out of the LD class. Ms. Woods transferred me in spite of my qualms. I remember sitting in the back of the class afraid that she would call on me to read. I was afraid that the big athlete would be found out for what he was, but Ms. Woods took a delicate approach with me.

I did quite badly on many assignments, and I flunked many tests. Then one day, Ms. Woods had this bright idea that she would have an essay contest and would have everyone write out what it is that they wanted to be and what they wanted to do with their life. I wrote out my goals and objectives of wanting to get my mom out of the ghetto and wanting to have a family. I had many dreams of having a nice house and car. I had dreams of not ever having to go to bed hungry. I thought about not having to have hand-me-down clothes, and about not having to have children who would be embarrassed about what kind of cars their parents drove.

We had a 1959 Cadillac that looked like the bat mobile and sounded like an old rugged truck, which embarrassed me when my parents used to drop me off in front of the school. I was embarrassed about having to wear the same clothes everyday too, and I was embarrassed about the level of mediocrity that had become so commonplace in my life.

Ms. Woods read all those words that I had written, and maybe it touched her; but she gave fifty dollars to the winner, and you got it, I won. This was the first time that I had won anything even remotely related to academics, and something happened to me when that took place. Ms. Woods also had a certain level of expectation of me after this, and she would no longer allow me to turn in mediocre papers. I remember that I flunked out on one of my spelling tests, and Ms. Woods called me up in front of the whole class and made me repeat: Good, better and best. Never let them rest. Until your good is better and your better is best.

She then said, "You are not a dumb jock Mr. Johnson, and you can do better."

I was embarrassed, and I wouldn't repeat that last pronouncement, or even the first one now, so she sent me to the office, where Coach Newhouse and the principal and Ms. Woods all met.

My Uncle used to always tell me that this situation was a conspiracy against the black man to keep the black man down, and that's why all those people met. But Coach Newhouse was my coach, and I loved him. Ms. Woods, even though I thought she was crazy, had a strange way of letting me know that she cared about me too. The principal was just one of those guys that, regardless of how tough he was, you just knew he had your best interest in his heart. Coach Newhouse told me that I needed to shut my mouth and get back down there and do whatever that woman told me to do.

Coach Newhouse was that coach that picked me up and fed me. He provided all of my athletic equipment so that I would be able to participate in all the sports in which I wanted to participate. In short, he was like my father. So, reluctantly, I shut my mouth and walked back down to the class, and in front of the whole class I recited, "Good, better and best. Never let them rest, until my good becomes better and my better becomes best. 'I am not a dumb jock, and I can do better.' I was happy when she told me I could sit down.

A couple of days went by, and we took another test. This time, I didn't make an "F" but a "D." I found myself once again up in front of the class and reciting the same words.

But then Ms. Woods said, "Put this in there too: I need an "A" to play."

I was mad again, upset, screaming in front of the class, "You just can't change the rules, Ms. Woods." And she told me to be quiet and that I could not play football until I got an "A."

I called Coach Newhouse, and he told me, "Well, I guess you better get an A." That Friday, I was not allowed to play in the game. I was very upset with Ms. Woods, but I was only angry because she was trying to pull me up and I was just lazy, trying to take the easy way out. Something clicked in me though.

Back in the class on Monday she said, "How did you enjoy the game Mr. Johnson?"

You got it. I was going to prove her wrong. I had the mentality that I was going to shut Ms. Woods up, and in front of the class. I decided that I was going to make her look bad by getting an "A" in her class. Who was playing whom?

So sure enough, I took my books home, after I found them in my locker underneath some clothes. I wrote those spelling words at least a hundred times a piece and knew them inside and out. I had memorized them, and when the time came to take my test, you got it, I made an "A." This was the first time I had made an "A" in English, or in any other subject for that matter. Ms. Woods, after grading my test, just put it at the bottom of the stack as if nothing big had happened. And I was like, "Oh no, you are gonna acknowledge my test!"

So I raised my hand, and Ms. Woods said calmly, "Mr. Johnson, may I help you?"

And I said, "You aren't gonna say anything about my test?" She said,

"Come on up, Mr. Johnson, and let the class hear what you have got to say."

So I stepped up in front of the class and my big man walk was shining. "Good, better, and best. Never let them rest, until my good becomes better and my better becomes best. I'm not a dumb jock, and I did better. I got my "A" so I can play."

Ms. Woods said, "One more thing Mr. Johnson, put this in there too, …in all my classes."

Ms. Woods had gone to all my other teachers and they were now in on the conspiracy, and it is a blessing when there is a conspiracy of great dream builders to pull us up, who will not allow us to accept mediocrity. They are conspiring for our help and for our hope. So many people are trying to take the easy way out, and the Ms. Woods, and Coach Newhouses of our world are the ones trying to pull us up, even when we don't want to get up. Because of Ms. Woods, I began a journey, and more importantly I really began to believe that I was more than just a dumb jock and that I could literally do better. In fact, as a result of this conspiracy, I did begin to do better. Do you have anyone in your life pulling you up, someone you are thinking is trying to pull you down? Well, you better stop and praise God that He sent somebody by to remind you of who you really are or who you can become. Sometimes you have to pull even when the one you're pulling don't want to be pulled.

Daddy Knew Best In This Case

My baby girl, as I stated earlier, has always been very tall. In the eighth grade, she was cheerleading and was about six feet tall at the time. I came to understand that there haven't been very many six foot-tall cheerleaders, not only in high school but also in college. She had not yet mastered the back flip which was mandatory to be a cheerleader and was beginning to get somewhat frustrated. Though she loved cheering and her whole social circle was cheering, I tried to motivate her to get involved in some other form of athletics. We really didn't push her toward basketball because Della and I felt it wasn't a good fit for her personality.

After a high school basketball game my family was attending Ki Ki Joseph, Director of Pike Youth Volleyball Club, walked up to us and asked why Kristina wasn't playing sports and invited Kristina to attend a volleyball clinic. The lights went on, but Kristina had this disgusted look on her face as if to say, "Volleyball, I don't want to play volleyball!" I asked Ki Ki about the league and she told us it was designed for beginners and was already in session and was interested in Kristina learning the game. I told her that Kristina would be there the next practice.

As you might imagine, especially if you have ever had a teen daughter, we had turmoil in the house. Kristina wouldn't talk to me and was pouting.

She asked how could I make her do something that she didn't want to do? She told me that I couldn't run her life and it was none of my business what she wanted to do. The only thing I could think about was, you are gonna play. I am going to pull you up even though you don't want to get up. My wife went along reluctantly at first. It was one of those times that I had to make a decision regarding what I felt was best, even though she didn't understand.

During the pouting time, Della went to Kristina and expressed to her to give volleyball her best and if she didn't like it at the end of the session she would go to dad and tell him and she would try another sport. Again she had my back.

The first day of practice, she took to volleyball like a fish to water. She could jump naturally, but the training she had in tumbling and jumping and flipping for cheerleading also assisted her in what she had to do in volleyball. Serving came naturally as well, as did playing at the net. A lot of the things that she had learned elsewhere just gravitated right to volleyball, and she had instant success. Her confidence began to build. That year, her ninth grade year, she started on junior varsity and had some time on varsity. We put her in club ball that year, which was our first exposure to the club ball scene — the tournaments and the traveling and all the expense that goes along with being on another level, doing things with your kids. But my daughter blossomed tremendously.

Volleyball has truly become her passion. She begged us to put up a volleyball net in the backyard for her to practice serves, etc., and she dragged us all over the country to watch college matches and professional women's volleyball matches. She recorded games and watched the tapes religiously and searched the web to see who the up and coming stars were and their stats. Many universities around the country recruited her and she's now a Gator!!! She accepted a scholarship to attend the University of Florida in Gainesville. She is a tremendous 3.8 student, and she is 6'3" now and all she wants to do is play volleyball. And one day you are going to be reading about my baby girl, Kristina, because one day, somebody pulled her up when she didn't want to get up. That's right, pull them up, even when they don't want to get up.

The bottom line, face it, is that no one owes you a living. What you achieve or fail to achieve in your life is directly related to what you do or fail to do. No one can choose his parents or his childhood, but you can choose your direction. Everyone has problems and obstacles to overcome that are relative to each individual, but nothing is carved in stone. You can change anything in your life if you want to badly enough. Excuses are for losers. Those who take responsibility for their lives are the real winners in life. Winners meet life's challenges head on, knowing there are no guarantees, and give it all they have. They never think it is too late or too early to begin. Time plays no favorites and will pass whether you act or not. So take control of your life, dare to dream and take risks, compete, and if you aren't willing to work for your goals, don't expect others to do so either. Believe in yourself, because God does. Believe you can soar!!

CHAPTER THIRTEEN

Just a Little Push

"Let us consider how we may spur one another on toward love and good deeds."

Hebrews 10:24

Not only did the little eagle in the coop need to be pulled up out of his bondage, but once he was at another level, free, he also needed to be pushed in order to become what he was supposed to be, pushed to yet another level. The little eagle, after arguing with the big eagle, was pushed off the cliff, and as he descended, screaming, "I am going to die." The wind caught his wings and miraculously the very thing that he thought would destroy him was the very thing that elevated him to go to another level.

I love this part of the story, for I am a part of the fellowship of the unashamed and I have the Holy Spirit's power. The die has been cast. I have stepped over the line; the decision has been made and I am a disciple of Jesus Christ. I won't look away, let up, slow down, back away, or be still. My past is redeemed, my present makes sense, and my future is secured. I am finished and done with low living, slight walking, small planning, chintzy giving and dwarf goals. I no longer need preeminence, prosperity, promotion, and positions of popularity. I don't have to be right, first, top, recognized, praised, regarded or rewarded. And I live by presence, learn by faith, walk by patience, live by prayer and labor by the power of God. My face is set, my grit is fast, my goal is Heaven, my road is narrow, my way is rough, and my reliable companion is my God. I am out of the coop and souring with the eagles on my way to eternity with the Lord.

My mission is clear. I cannot be bought, compromised, deterred, lured away, turned back, deluded or delayed. I will not flinch in the face of sacrifice, hesitate in the presence of adversity, negotiate at the table of the enemy, ponder at the pool of popularity, or linger in the maze of mediocrity. I won't give up, shut up, or let up until I have stayed up, stored up, preached up and paid up for the cause of Christ. I am a disciple of Jesus Christ, and I must go until His return. And when He comes to get His own, He will have no problem recognizing me. My colors will be very clear. I will be washed in crimson red, because I am a disciple of Jesus Christ.

To be a disciple one must be disciplined, which is a lost art in our society today — no one wants to sacrifice for anything. But it is the discipline that brings about the restraint in our life, and it is the adversity and pressure that allows us to fly. "Therefore, go and make disciples of all nations, baptizing them in the name of the Father and of the Son and of the Holy Spirit" (Matt 28:19). To make disciples, disciplined people who follow after the precepts of the Lord, is a tedious process. But the mandate that we have been given by God, to literally speak into existence to help Him to render those unto him who are his creation, to help Him to develop those who will follow after us: to push, to spur, to give assistance. "My son, do not despise the Lord's discipline and do not resist his rebuke. Because the Lord disciplines those whom he loves. As a Father, the son he delights himself in" (Prov. 3:11-12).

One of my favorite scriptures is, "Whoever loves discipline, loves knowledge, but whoever despises correction is stupid." That's where I get the terminology, "Don't be *stuck on stupid*," from Prov 12:1. So many young people and even adults feel discipline is a negative. Over and over in scripture God tells us this is a lie. Discipline in all phases of one's life is a must.

I tell my son, Kendall, all the time: you are what programs you. We are fighting for more than just us. As African Americans in particular, there are problems that have been passed down from one generation to another. In the inner city, 90% of families have single mothers as the head of the household. We have more black men in prison than in college. Because 90% of all babies born to black teenage mothers are born out of wedlock, gangs are providing alternative families. Thousands of black young men have died in the streets because of insensitive violence. In fact, 72% of all homicide victims are between the ages of 18 and 39, and 90% of them are black. Furthermore, 6 out of 10 black children grow up without a father. We must push to break the cycle of abandonment and hopelessness. Other communities certainly matter to me, but I take these terrible statistics personally as a black man and vow to fight against the devil who is trying to destroy our community. The evil one is trying to destroy the legacy that we can live and leave for our children. I started with Kendall, to raise him up and not exasperate him. Scripture tells me that fathers are not to exasperate their children, but to bring them up in the training and instruction of the Lord (Eph. 6:4).

I started this book years ago, as many of these stories are put together to leave for my children. The book is something that I can give to them that might give them some insight. It has just grown into what you are reading now. I realized that my story could have an impact on other lives then just my own family. I was thinking more like a chicken then eagle.

Children are my passion. I came across this poem, and it kind of shook me, explaining as it does some of our children's plight, particularly in school.

The New School Prayer

Now I sit me down in school
Where praying is against the rule
For this great nation under GOD
Finds mention of him very odd.
If scripture now the class recites,
It violates the Bill of Rights.
And anytime my head I bow
Becomes a Federal matter now.
The law is specific, the law is precise.
Prayers spoken aloud are a serious vice
For praying in a public hall
Might offend someone with no faith at all,
In silence alone we must meditate,

God's name is prohibited by the state.
We're allowed to cuss and dress like freaks,
And pierce our noses, tongues and cheeks.
They've outlawed guns, but first the BIBLE.
To quote the Good Book makes me liable
We can elect a pregnant Senior Queen,
And the 'unwed daddy,' our Senior King.
It's "inappropriate" to teach right from wrong,
We're taught that such "judgments" do not belong.
We can get our condoms and birth control,
Study witchcraft, vampires and totem poles.
But the Ten Commandments are not allowed,
No word of God must reach this crowd.
It's scary here I must confess,
When chaos reigns the schools a mess.
So, Lord, this silent plea I make
"That if I should be shot at my school today
I pray of Lord my soul you'll take!"

Written by a teenage sister in Baghdad, AZ

Yes, this does depict all the shootings at Columbine high school in Colorado, and the ruthless shootings in Arkansas, Texas, and in other areas of the United States where violence seems to be running rampant because children do what they are programmed to do. We as community leaders, teachers, parents and mentors must take responsibility and begin to acknowledge what we can do to prevent this from happening in the future and to provide positive examples that kids can reference to help them with their life choices.

Let's look at a group in our society. Young black boys and why so many of them feel and act the way they do. Slavery plays a big part in understanding the mentality of why young African American men in particular act the way that they do.

Ephesians 5:22-29 talks about the relationships between husbands and wives. However, verse 28 is a key verse that we must concentrate on. In the same way that "husbands are to love their wives as their own body…, and he who loves his wife, loves himself," so all humanity is to love each other as we love ourselves. One of the key elements that we must understand that has descended to us from slavery is this problem of devaluing one's self. Before one can change one's actions, one must clarify one's identity.

We were told during slavery that we were nothing more than breeders. We were stripped from our title of leaders and forced to impregnate women and not take responsibility for our actions. We were taught that our lot in life was to be subordinate to every other man. We were trained not to look white men in the eyes, to look down or to look away. We were taught after slavery that we would be the first fired and the last hired.

Many things have been passed on from one African-American generation to another, and many of those gifts were good — but many more were not. Even if a man got haughty and arrogant and thought that he would run away, the mothers, in an attempt to protect them, would encourage them to accept their lot in life. To this day, some black mothers see no problem with their sons dating two or three women at a time. They train their sons to do the very thing that they will not accept in their own relationships because of this long heritage.

I am amazed when I think of all the men who stand around on street corners talking, standing out in front of liquor stores for hours. Where did that come from? Well, during slavery, the breeders would stand around and talk about the conquests that they would have, of all the children that they had fathered. It gave them a sense of identity and purpose, status so to speak, and today that behavior is still passed on. We must break the cycle because only you can figure out why you act the way that you act and do the things that you do. Only you can change you, and then if, and only if, you identify with the freedom that you now have. Your identity is found in your relationship with the one who is now modeling behavior for you, providing you with leadership, guidance and direction. And this can only come from a mighty, awesome God.

Here are some things I want you to think about whether you are African American or not. One, what man or person has served as your role model as you were growing up? Two, what were their coping mechanisms; how did they handle stress? Three, what behavior did they model for you when they felt like they couldn't make it? Did they turn to alcohol, cocaine, and marijuana? Did they cuss? Did they hit someone? Were they fussing? Did they stay out late? Did they pray? The old saying is: "Like father, like son." Who has played a part in pushing you to be the best that you could be? If you have no one like this, can you be the model others will look to in the future?

He Looks Just Like You

One evening my son, Kendall and I were in a department store shopping. A sales clerk walked up to me and stated "this has to be your son, he looks just like you". I responded, "yes he is" as only a proud father would do. That is the greatest compliment you can give a father. My prayer and hope is that my son will follow after me as I follow Christ and that when people see him they will see the Father.

I believe I gave my daughter her passion for athletics and my son, Kendall, his passion for music. When I think about the day he was born and how much joy I felt when I held him in my arms, bringing him home from the hospital and dedicating him to the Lord and asking God to bless and keep him as a man of God. I remember the times he made messes in his diaper and as he got older the messes only got bigger and more expensive! You pay because success always comes with a price.

When Kendall was about two years old we noticed he would get spoons and pots and pans to imitate playing the drums. When we were at church he would stand and stare at the band during praise and worship and when the preaching began he would fall asleep. When the band began he would wake up and stare again. To say that music is his passion would be an understatement. Drum and piano lessons started at age seven. We've attended hundreds of recitals and band competitions. He took a stab at athletics but it wasn't in his heart. Della helped me understand that Kendall's heart was into music, he was doing sports because that's what I wanted for him. I had to let him follow his heart not mine in this case. Once he got into middle school he was a part of the Jazz Band and in high school he was in Concert Band, Jazz Band, Wind Ensemble and Marching Band. During his junior and senior year in high school Kendall was the drum line section leader.

You can find Kendall now playing drums for our church and is the leader of the teen praise team and band. He is writing Christian music that has a great impact on the young people he ministers to. Kendall will always be involved with music after furthering his education in music production.

- "Train up a child in the way that he should go, and when he is old, he will not depart from it" (Prov. 22:6).

- "I can do all things through Christ, who strengthens me" (Phil. 4:13).

- "Examine yourself, whether ye be in the faith. Prove your own self" (2 Cor. 13:5).

- "And the heart is deceitful above all things and desperately wicked, who can know it?" (Jer. 17:9).

These are all accountability scriptures that I use not only with the men I work with for the Indianapolis Colts and when I travel around speaking, but also with my son. My son and I have entered into an accountability time, where we hold one another accountable for scripture and the way that we conduct ourselves. Yes, my son. We started when he was 13 years old, asking him hard questions and modeling for him what he should be and the way that he should conduct himself. It says in 2 Peter 1:10 "Therefore my brother be all the more eager to make your calling and election sure. For if you do these things you shall never fail." What are these things? The things that God holds us accountable for. "And to your faith, add goodness; to goodness, knowledge; and to our knowledge, self-control; to our self-control, perseverance; to our perseverance, godliness; and to our godliness, brotherly kindness; and to our brotherly kindness, love. And love covers a multitude of sins." I am trying to train my son that love is more than just laying down with a woman. Love is more than just liking her for what she looks like or what she smells like. Love is commitment for the long haul.

So we ask each other these questions:

Question one: Do we spend time daily in scripture and prayer? A man that meditates on God's word is kept by that word. And how can a man keep his way pure? By meditating on God's word day and night. "Thy word is a lamp unto my feet and a light unto my path." It is the roadmap that guides us. It is the basic instruction before leaving earth — it is the BIBLE and we can do nothing without it and everything with it.

Question two: Have you had any flirtatious or lustful attitudes, tempting thoughts, or exposed yourself to any explicit material that would not glorify God? What goes in is what comes out. We as men respond sexually to visual stimulation. So I help guard what we watch, what we look at, for pornography on television and on the web is at an all-time high. Who do we have in our life to check on us regarding what we are exposing ourselves to? If only someone had checked David when he was up on that roof. Would David have committed adultery with Bathsheba if he would have known what it would bring about? Remember, he was the one who had said over and over again how he loved God's law. But it was breaking the ten commandments, coveting his neighbor's wife, that led David to commit adultery, thus breaking the 7th commandment. Then in order to steal his neighbor's wife, thereby breaking the 8th commandment, he committed murder and broke the 6th commandment. He broke the 9th commandment by bearing false witness against his brother. This all brought dishonor to his parents, thus breaking the 5th commandment. In this way, he broke all of the 10 commandments in relating to loving thy neighbor as thyself, commandments 5-10; and in doing so, he dishonored God, in effect breaking the first 4 commandments. Every time you are tempted to sin, you must ask yourself: "What's the price?" If David would have done that he probably wouldn't have sinned.

Question three: Have you been above reproach with your finances? Yes, we teach him about tithing even at his age. He must learn about saving and budgeting, about being responsible in the areas of finances. When we talk about training up a child, scripture is literally telling us what we do to create financial difficulties in our children's life that will save them from poverty. Particularly in the African American community, this is not stressed. Many do not stress the long-term benefits of discipline generally. Instead they stress instant gratification. Put it on credit, put it on layaway. And so they train their child with the mentality that will keep them in bondage. We need to owe no man anything but love. Live your life in such a way that you pay for everything in cash. How do you do that? That's the legacy that we try to pass on to our children.

Question four: Have you spent quality time in relationships with your friends and family? Quality and quantity are a thin line. As much as I am called to do around the country, keeping the balance of being provider and guider for our home is vitally important. We train our children by being available to our children. We have got to spend time with those we want to make an impact upon.

Question five: Have you done your 100% best in your job or school or etc.? Mediocrity is what we have been talking about throughout this book. You need someone in your life who is consistently pulling and pushing you to be the best that you can be, that caring Eagle to push you out of the coop. You also need to hold others accountable, not by what you ask them but by checking their own work. We check what they do because we respect what people inspect. And what people inspect we respect and we don't neglect. If you don't want your children or people in your life to be neglectful, inspect their lives. Examine them, help them to show themselves approved. Help them make their election and calling sure.

Question six: Have you told any half-truths or outright lies, putting yourself in a better light to those around you? Integrity is becoming a word that is not often times associated with manhood. Promise Keepers has taught us that we have to be men of our word. Let our yeas by yea, and our nays be nay. My son models not what he hears me say but what he sees me do, because what I do speaks louder than anything I can ever say. So never embellish, never stretch the truth because God wants men and women of integrity, of principle, men and women whose word can be counted on.

Question seven: Have you shared the gospel with an unbeliever this week so that we can spur one another on toward love and good deeds? That means that we have a responsibility to share the most important thing in our lives with other people. If God is the most important thing, why wouldn't we share Him?

Why wouldn't we want to allow someone else to experience the awesome majesty and power of the Savior? It shouldn't be a stretch to talk about the most important thing in your life. And if it is, then my question would be: Well, what is it the most important thing? If you won a million dollars in the lottery, you would have no problem sharing with people how blessed you were to have the luck that you have encountered. If you had experienced something that made you feel so much joy, you would literally want to have everyone else experience it. So, is the joy of the Lord your strength, or has Satan sifted it from you? We make a commitment every week to share the gospel with someone.

Question eight: Have you taken care of your body through daily physical exercise and through proper eating and sleeping habits? One of the things that I talk to children about who are *stuck on stupid* is the fact that they wear themselves out. People who are *stuck on stupid* don't think about this aspect of God's temple. Obesity is a very big problem in our society today. People overeat and it is a bad act of witness. People of God need to call it out and hold others accountable to what they put into their bodies. God only gives us one to take care of and to be a janitor of because he uses us to make a difference. If we can't properly manage ourselves in this society and in this world, we are ineffective players in this game of life. Therefore, God wants us to be in shape, not only spiritually but physically also. That's why I really stress not only my children but also to myself to take good physical care of God's temple, and so should you. If you are overweight, push back from the table and learn to fast, learn to discipline yourself and you will go a long way in life. Someone once said, "We should polish the brass of a sinking ship because it's your ship and it should look good while it is going down."

Question nine: Have you allowed any person or circumstance to rob you of your joy? I said earlier that the joy of the Lord is my strength. Satan can't take my joy; I have to give it to him. If someone spits on you, like my grandmother said, it doesn't make you mad, it just makes you wet. The offense is not the ultimate end. The offense is the trap, and Satan will try to steal your joy by offending you. When you take offense, anger takes place. And when anger comes in, that is when you sin. Don't allow any circumstance or person to offend you to the point that they make you angry. Shake it off and pack it under your feet.

Question ten: Have you lied to me on any of the questions that you answered today? That is vitally important, so check them. Go back sometimes to the previous questions, and be honest and deal with them with integrity.

I want you to ask yourself the following questions as well, including this important one: What makes you feel good about you?

Nurtured vs. Neglected

- Tell the truth and shame the devil is an old saying. Have you been disciplined enough by your parents, or are you/were you able to get away with murder?

- What makes you feel significant or important?

- What makes you feel secure and safe?

- Are you aware of any areas where you have not been properly nurtured, yes or no? And if it is yes, what are you doing about it?

- What one thing did your parents do to make you feel nurtured and loved?

- By answering these questions openly and honestly, you will begin to develop some insight. Where was/is your foundation? Who is equipping you to be the best that you can be?

Is it worth it?

I discussed earlier that we as men are tempted sexually by what we see. And I respond by asking the question: What is the price? Is it worth what we will have to pay for it? I tell my son all the time that we must have an internal video in our mind that we play back to ask ourselves this question: Is it worth it? And we need to answer this question not only from a negative perspective but from a positive perspective.

Let's start with the negative first. Let's say a man sees this woman that he is attracted to both physically and emotionally. She is pretty, very attractive, and he tells himself, "Oh man, I would really like to get with her; she would be real nice." But then he has to ask himself, is it worth it? So he plays the tape to fast forward to the worst case scenario. Men play different scenarios in their minds. Let's say he happened to get with her, and she gets pregnant. She calls his wife and tells her that he got her pregnant and that she is taking him to court. They go to court and find that he is the father of an illegitimate child while married. He has committed adultery. His children find out. The media finds out. His wife and children are embarrassed. His wife then decides to file for divorce. Therefore, he loses his home and his children. He loses all his self-dignity and respect. So he loses everything he worked for. His wife happens to meet someone else and they get married. The new husband moves into his house and begins raising his kids. He is paying child support, living in another home, another place somewhere. Yes, God could possibly restore him, and yes he could possibly move on. Think about this price, it is too high to pay for what he could gain with any

woman no matter how good she might look. A short-term decision causes him long-term negative consequences.

Now let's look at the positive and play the good tape. He
sees a woman he is attracted to both physical and emotionally.
She's pretty and attractive and he tells himself, she sure does
look good and she would make someone a nice wife but not me,
I have mine. God has blessed me with a wonderful wife who has
always had my back and loves me more than life itself. How can
I ever begin to think of giving up God's best for the schemes of
the devil? Nothing and no one can come between the commitment I have to her. I see myself growing old with her, raising
our children and seeing our grandchildren born and taking them
to Disneyworld. I visualize retiring in Florida playing golf and
coming home to my lovely wife who's been out shopping all day
for the grandkids. God is Good!

CHAPTER FOURTEEN

Never Quit: Time and Consistency

"For even when we were with you, we gave you this rule: if a man will not work, he will not eat

Thessalonians 3:10

"A patient man has great understanding, but a quick-tempered man displays folly"

Proverbs 14:29

Every worthy purpose takes time and consistency. Never, never, never quit!

Today there is a spirit that has invaded many people, that destroys any kind of work ethic. Everyone wants something for nothing: trying to hit the lottery, suing for any and every reason. Whatever happened to just working for what you need. "The price of success is hard work, dedication to the job at hand, and the determination that, whether we win or lose, we have applied the best of ourselves to the task at hand" (Vince Lombardi).

So many young people I've met think the world owes them something and I generally talk to them to let them know and give them ideas to understand what the bottom line really is. These next few pages are some of the presentation materials I use to impact young lives.

The Bottom Line

Face it, nobody owes you a living. What you achieve or fail to achieve in your lifetime is directly related to what you do, or fail to do. No one chooses his parents or childhood, but you can choose your own direction. Everyone has problems and obstacles to overcome, but that too is relative to each individual. Nothing is carved in stone. You can change anything in your life, if you want to badly enough. Excuses are for losers; those who take responsibility for their actions are the real winners in life. Winners meet life's challenges head on, knowing there are no guarantees, and give it all they've got. Never think it's too late or too early to begin. Time plays no favorites and will pass whether you act or not. Let God help you take control of your life. Dare to dream and take risks, compete. If you aren't willing to work for your goals, don't expect others to. Believe in yourself. God does.

Many of life's failures are men who did not realize how close they were to success when they gave up.

Procrastination is one of the major areas that not only stifles creativity but also hinders progress. This poem Mr. Meant-To expresses my sentiments better.

Mr. Meant-To

Mr. Meant-To has a comrade.
And his name is Didn't Do.
Have you ever chanced to meet them?
Have they ever called on you?
These two fellows live together
In the House of Never Win
And I'm told that it is haunted
By the ghost of Might Have Been.

Anonymous

There is so much great information God has put in his people's hearts and minds so that we can help one another overcome the desire to give up when things get hard. The key is to just pass it on. Like I stated earlier one of my favorite sayings is, it's not your aptitude but your attitude that determines your altitude, and only if you have persistence, courage, and fortitude will you reach as high as you can reach. I have talked about attitude and courage, so let's look at persistence. Nothing in the world can take the place of persistence. Talent will not; nothing is more common than unsuccessful men with talent. Genius will not; unrewarded genius is almost a proverb. Education will not; the world is full of educated derelicts. Persistence and determination alone are omnipotent. Persistence prevails when all else fails.

Persistence comes from the root word "persist" — to refuse to give up when faced with opposition or difficulty. We get the word persevere and perseverance from this same root.

"Therefore, since we have been justified through faith, we have peace with God through our Lord Jesus Christ — through whom we have gained access by faith into this grace in which we now stand. And we rejoice in the hope of the glory of God. Not only so, but we also rejoice in our suffering because we know that suffering produces perseverance, perseverance produces character, and character produces hope. And hope does not disappoint us, because God has poured out His love in our hearts by the Holy Spirit, whom He has given us." (Romans 5:1-5).

Whatever you have your faith in will shape your character. Your faith will determine what you value. Your values will determine your decisions and your decisions will shape your character. Faith is an unquestioning belief that does not require proof or evidence, an unquestioning belief in God (Hebrews 11:1). "Now faith is being sure of what we hope for and certain of what we do not see." "And without faith it is impossible to please God because anyone who comes to Him must believe that He exists and that he rewards those who earnestly seek him." (Hebrews 11:6). Values, the social principles, goals, or standards held or accepted by an individual, class, society, etc.

The Big Ten/The Ten Commandments! (From Exodus 20)

1. *Thou shalt have no other gods before me.*
2. *Thou shalt not make unto thee any graven image.*
3. *Thou shalt not take the name of the Lord thy God in vain.*
4. *Remember the Sabbath day to keep it holy.*
5. *Honor thy father and thy mother.*
6. *Thou shalt not kill.*
7. *Thou shalt not commit adultery.*
8. *Thou shalt not steal.*
9. *Thou shalt not bear false witness.*
10. *Thou shalt not covet.*

If we would live our lives by the Big Ten, our decisions would all be in order. Decision is defined as the act of deciding or settling a dispute or question; by giving a judgment; the act of making up one's mind. A judgment or conclusion reached or given. We need to base our decisions on God's Word. "I hate double-minded men, but I love your law." (Psalm 119:113). And a double-minded man is unstable in all his ways (James 1:8). We can't have our mind on God and on the world at the same time. It tells us in Romans 12:1-2 to renew our minds and not be conformed to the world.

Character, moral strength, self discipline, fortitude etc. are characteristics that are needed to be all that God has called us to be as well as to maintain a good reputation, and it is important what people who know you really think about you. For they know who you are when no one is looking, the person that talks back to you in the mirror. "Do not be misled: 'Bad company corrupts good character'" (I Corinthians 15:33). Who can find a wife of noble character? God has blessed me with two-in-one with my wife Della. She brings out the best in me, and with her beside me I feel I can do anything I put my mind to. She is also a woman of God and has great character. She is the mother of all mothers, lover, friend and prayer warrior. Who can find a wife of noble character, indeed. I did. Her name is Della Johnson.

The following story entitled The Meanest Mom depicts some of the characteristics Della has.

The Meanest Mom

As a child, I had the meanest Mother in the world. She was real mean. When other kids ate candy for breakfast, she made me eat cereal, eggs and toast. When other kids had Coke and candy for lunch, I had to eat a sandwich. As you can guess, my dinner, too, was different from other kids.

My Mother insisted on knowing where we were at all times. You'd think we were on a chain gang. She had to know who our friends were...and what we were doing. She insisted that if we said we'd be gone for an hour, that we would be for one hour less. She was real mean.

I am ashamed to admit it, but she actually had the nerve to break the child labor laws. She made us work. We had to wash the dishes, make all the beds, learn to cook, and all sorts of cruel things. I believe she lay awake nights thinking up mean things for us to do.

She always insisted on us telling the truth, the whole truth and nothing but the truth.

By the time we were teenagers she was much wiser, and our life became even more un-bearable. None of this tooting the horn of a car for us to come running. She embarrassed us no end by making our dates come to the front door to get us.

I forgot to mention, while my friends were dating at the mature age of 12 or 13, my old-fashioned Mother refused to let me date until I was 15 or 16. She was mean.

My mother was a complete failure as a mother.

None of us has never been arrested...or beaten a mate. Each of my brothers served his time in the service of his country...willingly, no protesting.

And whom do we have to blame for this

terrible way we turned out? You're right...our mean mother.

Look at all the things we missed. We never got to take part in a riot, never burned draft cards, or got to do a million and one things our friends did.

Our mean Mother made us grow up into God-fearing, educated, honest adults.

Using this as a background, I am trying to raise children. I stand a little taller and I am filled with pride when my children call me, "mean."

You see...I thank God he gave me the meanest mother in the world.

Author Unknown

If you have or work with children you know how challenging they can be. Constantly pulling and pushing them to be better than they want to be. We must never give up on them. The old preacher Samuel Procter states "a young persons mind is not cultivated enough to understand the consequences of their choices." We are the cultivators and part of cultivating starts with understanding that the ground you start with needs to be tilled. So when the tilling becomes difficult just think about the reward, a life that's changed for the better.

What is your faith in: money, fame, status, family, friends, spouse, job, appearance, giftedness or skills, etc? If it is in anything other than Christ, it will always let you down. Jesus is the only thing that will never change. Lord, I commit my plans to you because I want them to succeed, and I know I can't lose with what you give me to use. So, as we work to always do our best, let us not ever forget that "in his heart a man plans his course, but the Lord determines his steps" (Proverbs 16:9). What happens when your plans the way you think they should?

Do you become discouraged, frustrated, losing all hope? Here is an example of a man's life that when you examine it he could have become discouraged and quit but ultimately his persistence paid off.

At the age of 22, he failed in business. At the age of 23, he ran for Legislator and was defeated. At the age of 24, he again failed in business. At the age of 25, he was elected to the Legislature. At the age of 26, his sweetheart died. At the age of 27, he had a nervous breakdown. At the age of 29, he was defeated for Speaker. At the age of 31, he was defeated for Elector. At the age of 34, he was defeated for Congress. At the age of 37, he was elected to Congress. At age 39, he was defeated for Congress. At the age of 46, he was defeated for Senate. At the age of 47, he was defeated for Vice President of the United States. At the age of 51, he was elected President of the United States. That's the record of Abraham Lincoln. This shows that if you "Keep Kicking" you can make it.

Keep Kicking

Two frogs hopped into a can of cream
Or so I've heard it told.
The sides of the can were shiny and steep
The cream was deep and cold.
"Oh, what's the use?" Said number one,
"Tis fate-no help's around
Good-bye, my friend! Good by said world"
And weeping still, he drowned.
But number two of sterner stuff,
Dog paddled in surprise,
The while he wiped his creamy face
And dried his creamy eyes.
"I'll swim awhile, at least," he said
or so it has been said.

It wouldn't really help the world
If one more frog was dead.
An hour or two he kicked and swam
Not once he stopped to matter,
But kicked and swam, and swam and kicked
Then hopped out via butter.

Anonymous

Whatever obstacles you find yourself confronted with never, never, never quit, no matter how long it may take you. God can give you courage in falling, pain, danger, or trouble. Firmness of spirit is fortitude. "We must use time creatively and forever realize that the time is always ripe to do great things" (Martin Luther King).

The length of our days is seventy years or eighty if we have the strength. Yet the span is but trouble and sorrow for they quickly pass and we fly away (Psalms 90:10).

As I stated earlier my life is a journey but for this example I want to compare life to a football game. I have summed life into four quarters. The first quarter is from age 1 to 20, second quarter 20 to 40 years, half-time is 40, third quarter is 40 to 60 years and fourth quarter is 60 to 80, after 80 years you're in overtime. This book is my first two quarters of life and I am into my halftime experience moving into the third quarter.

There is a lot more on my journey still yet to be experienced and truly the best is yet to come! Can't wait to see what God will add to the 3rd and 4th quarters of my life!   MORE TO COME......